73/6

CHESTER COLLEGE LIBRARY

Author PETERS

Title Backpacking

Class No. 796.54   Acc. No. 79/1016

This book is to be returned on or before the last date stamped below

BACKPACKING

BACKPACKING

JAMIE PETERS

DAVID & CHARLES
Newton Abbot   London   North Pomfret (Vt)

Peters, Jamie
    Backpacking.
    1. Backpacking — Great Britain
    I. Title
    796.54   GV199.44.G7

    ISBN 0-7153-7966-6

Library of Congress Number
79-56581

Typeset by Photoprint, Paignton
and Printed in Great Britain
by A. Wheaton & Co Ltd Exeter
for David & Charles (Publishers) Limited
Brunel House Newton Abbot Devon

Published in the United States of America
by David & Charles Inc
North Pomfret Vermont 05053 USA

Contents

List of Illustrations

Introduction

For the uninitiated, 'backpacking' is 'lightweight camping', or, for the old-fashioned, hiking. It enables any fit person, for small capital expenditure, to have a glorious self-sufficient holiday. Backpacking is travelling by foot and surviving comfortably in the wild and beautiful parts of the country. Backpacking is walking in the hills for an unlimited period with everything you need in a rucksack on your back, and it is catching on. The available equipment has really advanced in the past year or so. There are numerous firms producing different ideas and putting them on the market at an amazing speed, so the choice of equipment is now very wide-ranging.

But why is backpacking becoming so popular? Why is tramping around in the pouring rain or on a six-inch thick white landscape, miles and miles from anywhere, so special? I think it is something to do with the need for a feeling of independence. In our normal lives we have everything conveniently to hand; we have cars to transport us and we have centrally heated homes to live in. In fact, we are supplied with every service you can think of, and in return we give a service ourselves by working. For many people this vicious circle has no sense in it, so, rather than fight it, which is almost impossible, they are getting away from the system by backpacking. To quote a rather comfort-loving backpacker:

'There's no limit to the pleasure you can derive from it.'

Backpacking is waking at first light with everything you need for breakfast at hand and popping your head out of the tent flap to the sight of a white and frost-bitten landscape in semi-darkness, with the morning mist obscuring the tops of the surrounding peaks . . . The breakfast brew and porridge water are boiling. After finishing the last spoonful of the porridge, you pack up and start the day's travels by walking into the sunrise, striding along without a care in the world because you know you have everything you need to survive comfortably on your back, and you don't need the world any more. From now on you eat when you want to, you stop when you want to, you take a different route because it looks interesting and because you want to — freedom at its most enjoyable. Sunset which signals the end of the day's travel and the pleasant tiredness of each and every exercised limb tells you it is about time you started looking for a pitch. Eventually, you find a spot which suits you and wearily set up camp and begin the evening meal. While sipping an after-dinner cup of coffee, you reflect back over the day's travel and events. Treasure those thoughts: you might need them when you are buried deep in industrial life one Monday morning.

With all the books on backpacking and equipment guides on the market telling you what to carry and what not to carry, you can soon see the old system creeping in again. Remember, nobody can tell you what to carry or what not to carry, what brand new ultra-lightweight tent to use or how to go backpacking. It's up to you and only you. Backpacking is utterly and completely personal.

Backpacking is something out of the ordinary, because it goes against everything in the system and, if you take up backpacking, you will probably be laughed at and suffer a few rude remarks from people who know no better, but I urge you to take everything that is thrown at you and to carry on walking through the hills and over the moors with your trusty pack because backpacking is fun and can bring no end of enjoyment. More important, it's an independent hobby: you don't have to rely on others for your own enjoyment.

Backpack now! You'll either like it or hate it and if you like it you'll be a backpacker for life, and you won't be sorry, I promise you.

1
Clothing

Most backpackers carry on their hobby all through the year and, what with this country's erratic and sometimes rather extreme weather conditions and temperatures, the backpacker has to try and keep at one temperature all through the year. He does this by insulating himself in winter and putting on as many layers of dry, woollen or specialist material garments as he possibly can, and in summer by ventilating himself. This is all very well until it starts to rain, and, believe you me, it will. Then he has to use something that will keep out the rain and, even more important, the wind. You can quite easily keep warm while wet, but the problem starts when breezes begin to blow and chill the wet body.

Boots and Socks

Boots are a very important part of the backpacker's equipment and they must fit just right, so always be careful of this before purchasing. The best backpacking boots are always made of leather with as little stitching as possible on the uppers; also feel for suppleness when buying as soft leather is best. Most backpacking boots have two tongues, the additional one being for comfort and to help the boot become watertight. The method of tying up boots varies somewhat, but my personal

Three 'D' rings enable boot laces to be released quickly

preference is three 'D' rings, with three hooks at the end for quick release. A lot of people think that splashing out about £50 on a pair of boots is the answer to successful footwear, and when they leak, get a surprise. But buying an expensive pair of boots is a waste of money unless you look after them. You can't do enough for your boots while they are not in use. Stage one is always keep them clean and stage two is to rub in leather preservatives with your own hand. Keep on and on doing this and the boot will become just like a soft glove and be a pleasure to wear when out hiking. Another good sign in a boot is the label on the sole: if it is yellow, then you know you've got nearly the best type of sole available on the market — a Montagna Vibram. Also, try the boot for ankle support. This is most important as lack of support could easily be the cause of a twisted ankle which might ruin a weekend, not to mention the pain that might be suffered. A good backpacking boot should not be too heavy either, but heavy enough to stop stones

Short gaiters or anklets protect socks from mud and water and prevent stones getting into boots

being felt through the sole or through the side of the boot. You might be interested in a little additional piece of handy gear I use in conjunction with my boots: they are short gaiters or anklets that fit over the top of the boot and around your ankles, the advantages being a waterproof seal around the top of the boots and a mud-protector for your socks and laces and, in particular, the knot in your laces, which can get caked up with mud and become difficult to undo. Top quality names for boots include Robert Lawrie, Scarpa, Hawkins and James Boylan.

Equally important for comfortable feet are the boots' partners and good friends — the backpacking socks. In general, wool, and only wool, socks will do. But I have used a mixture of wool and man-made material with great success, so I have no hesitation in recommending them. Socks should be dry and fluffy at all times though, and when they begin to lose that quality after a wash, then they are on their way out. Size is very important again, and an accurate fit is a must. As far as the amount of pairs worn or, if you like, an undersock, is concerned, this is completely personal, but I always have a nylon undersock because I am allergic to wool directly on my skin. I have a friend who is allergic to nylon on his feet, so it's just a matter of taste. Loopstitched socks are the very best for warmth; these socks are just stitched in loops rather than straight stitches and hold the heat very well.

Trousers

There are two types of backpacking trousers: one is the normal size and cut trouser, and the other is breeches, which are cut just below the knee. Either choice is personal, but it is a necessity to wear long socks with the breeches unless you want to show off your short, fat, hairy legs and freeze in the process! Over the years, I think my personal preference has just edged towards trousers, as you can always roll them up anytime and use them as breeches, but can also roll them down when the wind gets a bit mean.

Materials available are numerous, but make sure your trousers are wool-based for warmth and ruggedness and, as you will find out, wool always keeps you warm while wet, which is vitally important. Wool also dries out very quickly indeed. Another new material good for outdoor trousers is Halenca 70 per cent.

Other features in backpacking trousers should be large back pockets for storage of map while walking, and good-sized side pockets to slip your hands in when there is a frost about. I also prefer a buttoned fly, as zips are cold and nasty things when backpacking, and they are also prone to break easily and ruin a good pair of trousers. And believe me, if you are ever in a desperate position and the zip gets caught — well, don't blame me! Another tip is always wear a belt, then if the trouser fastening breaks, you are OK. I once had to wear a piece of string around my waist all weekend, and it's not funny when everybody you meet extracts something out of you by saying,

'Come from Dorset, do 'ee? Arrrr!' Recently, I have been wearing shorts all through the summer period and this is a really great way to walk. You are at complete ease and the most comfortable experience is savoured. You also get a great suntan too, whether the sun is shining or not.

Top Wear

If you don't mind wearing vests, then that is your best bet for the first garment on top, and, even better, if they are in string form and T-shirt design. Over that can either be a woollen jumper and then a climber's thick woollen shirt acting as a jacket or the woollen shirt first and a fibre-pile specialist jacket on top. The main consideration with top wear is that ventilation or insulation can be adjusted at a minute's notice, and to do this it is a good idea to have buttons or zips up the middle of every upper garment, so enabling you to keep the body temperature at roughly one level all the time, no matter what the weather does. Again, I like all my jackets to have large pockets on the sides and breast pockets. These are very handy for compasses, otherwise dangling and bumping about and causing irritation, pipes or cigarettes if you happen to like your baccy, and trail snacks.

Another feature on jackets which, in my view, is a must rather than an optional extra is a high-buttoned or zip-fastened collar. I realised the benefit of this a while ago when I was testing a new fibre garment in a chilly wind. The furry collar sealed off all my neck, right up to my chin. The advantage of this was immediately felt through sheer warmth and comfort.

Another very valuable advantage of a fibre-pile jacket is that, like wool, it makes very good insulation when it's wet. In the rain, I have often taken all but my undergarments off and put on my fibre jacket underneath waterproofs; it directly soaks up all condensation and eliminates that uncomfortable feeling which is always attached to wearing waterproofs in the normal

way; in fact, it is almost enjoyable wearing waterproofs in this
way, but the key is to take off nearly all other top wear, putting
them in your dry pack, and so preventing the heat from
building up.

Odds and ends which I had better mention under this heading include scarves, towels, cravats and any other objects
which you might care to sling around your neck. You will need
good draught protectors if you don't happen to have a collar.
Some people just like the feel of something around their neck.
A cravat can be very successfully substituted by a towel; in fact,
you might already have a proper towel around your neck
anyway. Other improvised neck wear might be a handkerchief,
dishcloth, emergency triangular bandage or sling shot for the
odd rabbit — no, I'm only kidding. Mind you, it's an idea,
though, isn't it?

Headgear and Gloves

Headgear and gloves are very important pieces of clothing,
believe you me. I have experienced walking in freezing cold
weather without gloves and, more important, without a woolly
hat, and the consequences were very nasty. I just could not get
warm in any way, and the strange part about it was that I had
enough other clothing to take on Everest. Afterwards I learnt
that a large amount of body-heat is lost through the head, so
when a chill is beginning to form put on a woolly hat, the
change in comfort is most noticeable. Headgear comes into its
own in the mornings and evenings when the temperatures are
at their lowest. In the mornings, when you have your first
argument with your sleeping bag (whether to get out for a pee
or stay with your bag!), is when you want your woolly hat, if
you win! It comes in handy also when you emerge from the
depths of the down to cook your fry-up. Just slip it on, and
there will be no drop in body temperature. When you start
walking in the morning, it is handy to have on for a couple of

miles to warm you up to travelling temperature. Another use for the woolly hat is under the hood of a waterproof: you may overheat slightly, but it is a comfort to know that no drips of water are going to run down your neck; also, the direct contact between head and nylon waterproof is eliminated. When you walk into your camp at dusk on a cold winter's afternoon and begin to pitch the tent, your woolly hat will be very welcome, and later on in the evening too, when you plod down to the pub or start a camp-fire and a chat.

Types of headgear vary, but I favour the fibre-pile balaclava. If you want it to be just a hat, then the neck piece folds inside the head part and you end up with a double layer of fibre around your head; when you put it fully into use, the whole of the head and well down the neck is completely sealed off, just leaving mouth, eyes and nose uncovered. Another practical type of hat is the Damart Thermo. This is particularly good for summer use, or for wearing under a waterproof. Many back-packers have different types of hats, and they seem something of a personal item to each individual. I have seen Scottish tar-tan hats, those French-type hats with the movable ear-pieces, hacking caps, football bobble-hats — the list would be endless. They are fun, though, aren't they?

I suppose I had better mention dark glasses. These are very important if you are to remain for any length of time in areas which have whited out. The higher you go up mountains, the more important they are, if snow-blindness is to be avoided.

Hand protection is very important to the hiker in winter, and mittens are far superior to gloves. Some backpackers carry waterproof mittens, in addition to the normal mitten, which is very wise, but lately gloves and mittens are being made out of fibre-pile, so if they get wet, your hands will still be kept warm, thus saving the weight of the waterproof ones. These gloves are also reasonably inexpensive.

A balaclava, woolly hat and mittens. In freezing weather it is important to stop heat loss, particularly through the head

Specialist Clothing

When you buy clothing to go backpacking in, you need go no further than Marks and Spencer or the local sports-camping shop, where everyday clothing, such as pure wool sweaters, woollen shirts, thick hard-wearing trousers, etc, are likely to be found, and these are quite ample to cover the needs of the average backpacker in average weather. But there will come a time when the equipment bug hits you, after you have progressed with your backpacking skills to winter hiking in mountains or moorlands, and you start thinking about specialist clothing, which is made especially for backpackers and climbers for the extreme conditions likely to be encountered in these parts. This is the time to pack backpacking in! No, I'm only joking. But it's when you get to this stage that you have to search deep, deep down into your pockets for that hard earned cash. Specialist clothing is very expensive. The best type, in my view, is a down-filled jacket.

Down has risen in price to an astronomical level and therefore is not within the grasp of the normal working man who takes to the hills at weekends. The reason that down is so expensive is something to do with China, which produces a good percentage of the stuff, and something to do with the dreaded inflation of this country — inflation, that awful word which always seems to hit the few people who want to enjoy themselves. Down is light and compresses into a very low bulk form; it is very warm. The only real disadvantage is that down loses its warmth when wet, so jackets must be worn under waterproofs when it is raining. If, by any chance, you can afford one, then I would suggest that you do invest in a very light one, because a lot of down jackets are too warm to walk in — they are that good. Down jackets are particularly good for wearing round camp at night and in the morning. Best makes in down clothing include 'Mountain Equipment' and 'Point-Five'.

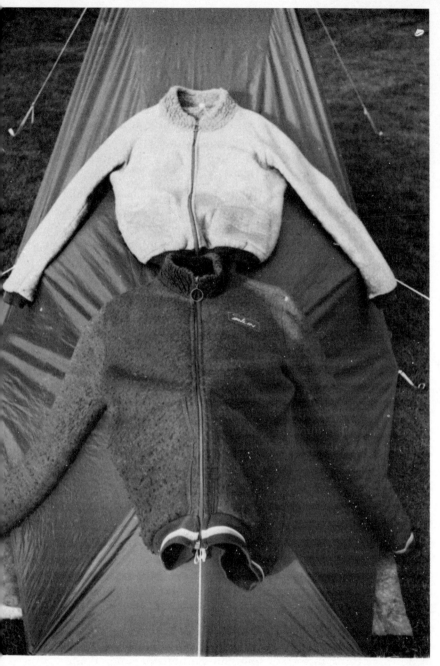

Fibre-pile jackets: the high 'wind-sealing' collar of the 'Javlin' (foreground) is a great asset

The most common specialist jacket seen amongst backpackers today is the fibre-pile garment. It is extremely popular
with the majority of backpackers and climbers, the reasons being that it is extremely good value for money, very warm, and
able to keep you warm while still wet. It is also reasonably hard-
wearing and smart-looking. The only snag is that it is bulky
when folded and when stuffed into a rucksack takes up an awful
lot of pack-space, but it is light. I wear it over a thick woollen
shirt, and this is my personal preference for clothing. One of
the advantages of this type of jacket is that it can double up as
bedwear and is extremely comfortable when worn next to the
skin. You can also get gloves, trousers and socks made in fibre
pile, the two latter are comfortable worn in bed and next to the
skin. The best name in these garments, in my view, is 'Helly-
Hansen'. They were also the original fibre-pile firm. Their
garments tend to be slightly harder-wearing than the rest.
Other names include 'Insulatawear', 'Javlin' and 'Tog 24'.
And don't forget the high 'wind-sealing' collar on these jackets,
which is a great asset.

The other type of specialist clothing, or more appropriately
specialist underwear, is called 'Thermowear'. The material is
extremely light and packs down nearly to nothing. It looks and
feels like very fine silk and works on the basis of direct and tight
contact with the skin. It is very comfortable to wear as
underwear or as pyjamas. In fact, a pair of thermowear pyjamas is all I need for most of the winter nights; really cold
nights, though, are supplemented by a fibre jacket. When you
put these pyjamas on to go to bed, don't be alarmed by the
sudden 'sparks' effect — it's just static electricity made by
brisk contact with the material. The first time this happened to
me, I didn't know whether I wanted a shave or a haircut until a
companion shouted over and commented on how pretty the
sparks from his pyjamas looked! Best makes include 'Helly-
Hansen Lifa Range' and 'Damart Thermo'.

Weatherproofs
(See separate chapter on Gore-tex)

I use the word 'weatherproofs' because it is not only rain we
need to keep out, but also wind. The two together produce the
most dangerous combination that is ever likely to be experienced by the backpacker, and that is a rapid decrease of heat in the
body's core leading to the serious risk of death from exposure.
A nylon waterproof fits this purpose more than amply. There is
no way the elements can get in if your garment is really totally
waterproof. Now for the snag: because nothing can get in, it
also works the other way — nothing can get out, including condensation or body moisture, which would normally have been
able to escape. What happens is that when your warm, damp
body air comes into contact with the inside of the waterproof
which is at a lower temperature, condensation takes place,
leaving droplets all over the inside of your weatherproof jacket.
This cannot be avoided, despite all the revolutionary claims of
companies who say they have a so-called 'breathable' waterproof (excluding one recent claim, which looks as though it has
really happened at last). Most of them are made of thick, oiled
cotton, which does breath, but is only waterproof for as long
as it takes the rain to soak through to the inner surface. Then
chilling takes place, which is no good at all. So really, all we
can do is to make life a little more comfortable inside. At least,
we are being protected from the main danger — the elements
— and that is the most important thing. All we can do is make
sure the weatherproof has a zip for ventilation and that we have
something on underneath which is going to keep us warm while
wet. It is rather uncomfortable wearing waterproofs at any
time — it's just a matter of putting up with them. Never be
tempted to take them off while it's still raining and blowing —
you'll end up in a worse position. Just have a sing-song or
something, and try to forget the discomfort; remember, you
can't appreciate life's good things unless you have experienced

some of life's worst. Just wait until you get in that sleeping bag after a day's walk in continuous rain; you'll think you have hit seventh heaven!

Waterproofed clothing comes in four basic designs: the one-piece cagoule, which has a slight opening at the top, but, in my opinion, not enough for proper ventilation; the zipped cagoule, which has a covered zip all the way down to the bottom — this is my choice; the waterproof leggings, which come with or without zip — again, I prefer a zip for ventilation; and, lastly, the rain chaps, which are just lengthened garters, really. These are very good, because they leave the crutch area free from direct contact with the waterproofs. A long cagoule to cover that part is necessary if chaps are to be worn though. I'm sorry — there are five basic designs — I have forgotten to mention the one and only controversial 'Saunders Pakjak', which is a waterproof cape with a built in pack cover. It is very baggy and through the pack cover you have no direct waterproof contact with your back, so as you can imagine, it does cut down condensation; the theory is excellent, but somehow it has never worked out for me. One day I was using it — the very first time, in fact — and it started to drizzle, one of those days when the weather couldn't make up its mind what it wanted to do. Well, I decided that I would put it on. By the time I actually got it on properly, it had stopped raining! And there was my friend watching the whole procedure, not attempting to get out his waterproof, but just with a grin on his face. After I had packed it away — it took about five to ten minutes — he just turned to me and said, 'If the Pakjak causes that much trouble, and takes as long as that to put on, I think I will give it a miss'. I could not reply. Ever since then, I have given the Pakjak a miss myself! If you do happen to get one on, it also has a slight similarity to, and the same effect as, a hang-glider. When there is a good wind about, you are likely to be launched into mid-air.

Good features in waterproofs include a large cut to increase ventilation; flap-covered pockets, well-sealed — as pockets tend to fill up with water, when it is raining; Velcro-covered zips; corded bottom and hood to seal off weather; taped seams in the inside of the garment; very small underarm vents to increase ventilation; and, lastly, a general good-quality look to it — it's well worth spending a bit on a good weatherproof, because it will then serve you well for many years.

2
Equipment for Camp

Somebody once said backpacking is mainly camping with walking as seconds. Admittedly, the overnight stop is very important as this singles out a backpacker from an ordinary walker. When night falls, the day walker turns to the shower, bar and comfortable bed for his enjoyment and shelter, while the backpacker, in love with his way of life, prefers the romantic setting of tent and sunset over a distant mountain. The whole idea of backpacking, in my view, is to travel with an aiming point in mind over a period of time, the longer the better. To do this successfully, he must be able to set up camp wherever he feels the need to recharge his batteries for the next stage.

Both walking and camping supplement each other; without the combination we would not have backpacking, both stages are as important as each other. So the aim of camp is a comfortable night's sleep and, to this end, the tent and pitch must be in good state to withstand any nasty happenings in the middle of the night, including low temperatures.

Tents
(See chapter on Gore-tex)

Some backpackers in summer use plastic bags as tents claiming that they are lighter than a tent and just as comfortable. I bought one of these 'bivvy' bags a while ago just to take along as a precaution against an emergency that might crop up. When I got back from that trip I weighed it — 1 ¾ lb. The advantages of this are that you probably lose about a pound in weight and the cost of a bivvy bag is next to nothing compared to a tent.

The disadvantages though are numerous. Severe condensation occurs causing acute discomfort leading to loss of sleep. There is a lack of cooking space and when it is raining, heaven knows where you cook. I can never understand the freaky types who use this method. They seem to hump these bags in the mountains without realising that for an extra pound or so in weight they could be getting oodles and oodles more comfort. Fair enough if they can't afford a tent, and I admire them for what they are doing; at least they are getting out and certainly they shouldn't stop going into the hills just because I don't like these bags, but surely if you intend to take backpacking seriously, a tent is a sound investment. In my opinion the plastic bivvy bag should only be used as an emergency shelter in case of freak weather conditions, but certainly not as a tent.

So we've decided, or rather I have decided, that a proper tent which stands is the best type of shelter. The sole materials used for these tents are either cotton or nylon. The advantages of cotton are that it can dispose of condensation through the wall of the tent, so leaving no signs of water on the inside of the tent. Also, the stitched seams of a cotton tent expand when they are wet so cutting out leakage altogether.

The disadvantages, however, are that cotton, although very heavy anyway, soaks up water and adds to the already excessive weight penalty. I think that everybody in backpacking and everybody involved in camping generally have slowly become accustomed to the more modern and more practical material of nylon.

These nylon lightweight tents come in two types: single-skin and double-skinned. Now that we are dealing with nylon tents and appreciate the advantages of low weight and bulk, we have to put up with the main sole disadvantage which is our good, or rather bad, old friend — the condensation phenomenon. This problem concerns the single-skin tent more than the double-skin, and mainly occurs when the outside temperature is much lower than the inside temperature of the tent. Then, if the wind gets up, the occupant will receive the full shower effect.

Single-skinned tents have their advantages too; they are at their best in summer when the temperatures are not so severe and the doors are able to be left open, so virtually cutting condensation out altogether. This is an extremely healthy way to sleep so long as you are warm enough and, of course, the weight advantage over doubles becomes an asset too.

Now to the pros and cons of a double-skinned nylon backpacking tent. The main disadvantages are that the weight is going to be slightly increased with the inner as an addition, but today the inner tents of an average tent are made out of extremely lightweight material so that's nothing major to worry about. The other disadvantage is that when pitching some double-skinned tents they need to be pitched inner first, so risking a severe soaking if it is raining. Usually it is quite easy though to modify the inners of such tents so that they can be erected after the fly is pitched, so saving a wetting.

The advantages of double-skinned tents are plenty, and they are probably the most popular all-round backpacking tent. First of all, you gain a notable improvement of temperature through good insulation which results from having two layers instead of one. The condensation problem is also cut to a minimum; this is achieved by a so-called breathable inner tent which is fine and very smooth to touch on the outer surface. It allows the damp air to pass through it and this then does not condense until it reaches the inner surface of the flysheet, then hopefully, rolling to the bottom of the tent on to the ground and out of danger. If any drips do fall on to the inner, the smooth outer surface should cause them to drain down to the bottom.

Another advantage with a double tent is that in summer you need only use the flysheet and when winter comes you just add your inner tent again, using it as an all-year-round tent.

Good features in lightweight tents include:

1 Good, strong, but light poles. It is important that poles can withstand severe winds. Failure of poles would lead to the tent falling down no matter how good the tent was. Try to get nesting poles which telescope inside each other rather than a big bundle of poles, so saving bulk and improving manageability. If faced with the choice of a single pole or A-Poles, always opt for the A-Poles so long as the weight is not too excessive.

2 General good quality. You can always tell a good tent by looking at the stitches and general finishing. The stitches should be in a dead straight line with a reasonable count to the inch and the tent should stand tight and erect, when pitched, not baggy and sagging!

3 The tent should have a fairly rough ground sheet with a tray effect and the edges should come well up the sides of the inner — the higher the better — in case of flooding or mini streams directed at the tent. I have often spent the night with water running under my ground sheet and would have been forced to evacuate if it were not for my deep-trayed groundsheet.

4 Good tents also have reinforced areas where the pole rests against the tent material, either by double stitching another piece of material in the area or by sewing in a leather patch. Also guy points ought to be of double strength and careful positioning of these points is important too.

5 Odd features include a down-opening A-Zip on the inner of the lightweight tent, so as to completely cut out all draughts. Banana-shaped guys, although this is only personal; the banana guy holds better than the locking guy, I find. Lastly, colour: obviously, if you want to be seen then, fair enough, buy a bright orange tent, but I can't see any reason for wanting to be seen. If you're a naturalist, surely the choice would be green and, in my view, that's the whole idea of backpacking, to get away from people and to blend in and become part of the country. People argue this point and say that they like to be seen in the mountains in case of an emergency. This is acceptable for parties of school children, but

surely you should not be out in the mountains if you are not confident of yourself and your personal skills. Besides, if the mist comes
down anyway, which is the most likely happening in mountain
areas, the rescuers will not be able to see ten yards in front of them,
let alone an orange tent miles away on the other side of the hill. It's
a point to think about, isn't it?

A 'tray' ground sheet

Just a quick last thought on not so much a feature of a tent,
but something that in my view needs to be done to every new
lightweight tent and that is to seal all the seams. Wherever
seams have been sewn, a needle has punctured the nylon, it
can't be helped, but I personally always carefully and
thoroughly seal every seam, including where the zip is sewn on,
and that then ensures 100 per cent water-tightness and no
leakage whatsoever.

Tent Shapes and Designs

There are so many different shapes and designs of tent that I
will have to use numbers again to explain every shape and
design differently so as not to confuse you, or rather so as not to
confuse myself!

A wedge tent supported by A-poles

1   THE ORDINARY WEDGE

The ordinary wedge shape was the original shape used for the first lightweight and mountain tent. It has extremely good wind-cutting ability due to its wind resistant edges. It is still the design used for the standard mountain tent even today, and the well-proven and loved Vango has become extremely popular with mountain campers. It can be used with either single upright poles at both ends or A-Poles, the latter being the choice of the mountain users. Through using this method, entry and exit is very easy and grovelling around the pole in the middle is avoided.

2   THE LONG-SIDED WEDGE

The first tent of this design to arrive on the market was the Karrimor single-skin Marathon Mark II. Using just two upright poles in the front of the tent and letting the flat back filter away into a tail, this tent was an extremely good wind tent and still is. It is the sort of tent you can put up anywhere. Later on, other firms as well as Karrimor improved on the design and made an all-round more comfortable tent using the old design to build on. What they did was to make the tent slightly bigger, give it two skins and also give it two back poles to make it even more stable — this was a great success.

3   THE HALF-BREED TENT

So at that time basically we had just those two designs. The more modern, double-skin, long-sided wedge and the good, old, faithful, original wedge. There were other odd designs like the hoop tent and the single-pole tent, but they never really caught on with backpackers. Then arrived a sort of half-breed tent using both designs and all the best features of the standing two. Unknown to me at the time, this tent was to become the nearest thing to *the* backpackers' tent.

A firm called Ultimate brought the new-look tent out and made a big mistake by not taking out a patent. Firms copied the design, but still today Ultimate make the best tent of this type by a long way.

The tent in question is called the Ultimate Solo. I have no hesitation in saying that I think this tent is nothing less than fantastic and that it is the best all-round solo mountain tent for backpackers available in this country today. Go out and buy one now!

The design briefly consists of two poles in the front joined together by a ridge pole and one pole at the back with the top panel tapering back towards the single pole. The front entry is

The Marathon Mark III

very easy because of no blockage by any single pole and the room is just ample and it is exactly where you want it; no room is wasted. You can probably imagine the wind stability of this tent, what with a near-square frame at the front and an ample, single back pole, it acts very well when it starts to blow. The quality of the tent is extremely high. The whole lot weighs 3lb 11oz.

When this tent came out I was lucky enough to be given one to test and a complete report by me appeared at that time in my column in *Camping Caravan Monthly*. The test report goes into a lot more detail about the tent. My views have not changed and therefore I have decided to include this in the next section. I hope you find it interesting. Just a quick word though about buying tents; don't rush into anything and remember that the more you pay the better the tent will be. It is no good taking short cuts and buying a Sunday-paper reduced-for-quick-sale bargain for £10 because it will not be worth it.

Remember, when you are out pitched on a mountain, you might just regret that bit of money saved and wish you had invested in something worth while.

U7/1 Solo from Ultimate Equipment

Lightweight tents in the past have been generally notorious for their lack of resistance to strong winds. Hence, U7/1 Solo, a new lightweight tent from Ultimate Equipment. Believe me, this one has all the ability needed to withstand any type of weather that our erratic British climate likes to throw at it. And it does this at a low weight and bulk level.

The four main features that a lightweight tent must have to be an ideal unit are as follows:

SIMPLE AND FLY: FIRST ERECTION

The tent instructions which I received with my test unit said

that the inner is erected first, but in my view, the flysheet must go up first, then erecting the inner can be done under shelter — an important point in bad weather.

First of all, you peg the back two peg points across the fly-sheet into the wind; then the very back peg, so that you get a V-shape on the ground; then the two front peg points at the widest part of the tent are pegged down; then all the peg points are pegged down except the middle two, halfway down the fly-sheet. Once this is done, the two front poles and the ridge pole can be put up. The ridge pole is threaded through the velcro-fastened loops at the top of the fly, then connected to the poles by two aluminium connectors. The poles are raised into position simultaneously. Pegging the guys of the fly sheet holds the tent up for the back pole to be put in. Crawl to the back of the fly and push the spike up through the spike hole in the fly remembering to attach the inner connecting tape first. Guy the back pole out. Adjusting and pegging all points tightly completes the erection of the flysheet.

Erecting the inner is an easy operation of pegging the ground sheet down and hooking the inner on to the poles which is all done under the shelter and, of course, in this way the inner stays completely dry.

The flysheet is a few inches away from the ground when pitched and this allows a circulation of air between the fly and inner at all times and, of course, this cuts down the probability of condensation occurring. On one of my test outings with the U7/1, a friend and I were pitched on the banks of a stream, the surrounding area of which was semi-wooded. It was also very damp and misty that night. Just a night for condensation I thought. In the morning, the bottom of my sleeping bag was slightly damp where it had been touching the tent in the night, but apart from that, the inner was completely dry.

WEATHER-BEATING ABILITY

The way the U7/1 Solo is constructed, I think it is fair to say that it has something that most lightweight tents lack, and that is the ability to withstand strong winds. You can actually sleep in this number without being constantly interrupted by a continual flap or thud. The double-pole ridge-pole front helps a great deal in high winds and although nylon is totally waterproof, it is advisable to seal all the seams, especially if the nylon tent is pulled taut, since this tends to open up all the stitch holes.

As far as weather beating is concerned, I think it would be pretty safe to take it nearly anywhere in the British hills and be confident that it would withstand nearly anything that is thrown at it weatherwise.

MAXIMUM ROOM WHERE NEEDED

The U7/1 Solo is strictly a one-man unit (hence, the 'solo'), but the tent seems to have more than enough room where it is needed. There is enough room between the inner and outer for the largest of pack frames to fit round for storage, and that leaves the large front bell end for cooking and storage. There is enough height at the front of the inner to sit up in, and entry and exit is very easy, which is a blessing, as with most lightweight tents you have to grovel round a pole to get in and out.

MINIMUM WEIGHT AND BULK

All told, the weight, including flysheet, inner, poles and connectors, guys and pegs, is 3lb 11oz. That is a very low weight for the protection you are getting. The unit comes in three bags — one for the poles, one for the inner and pegs and one for the flysheet — and all are very low in bulk.

This new Ultimate tent is a winner in my view. It offers a

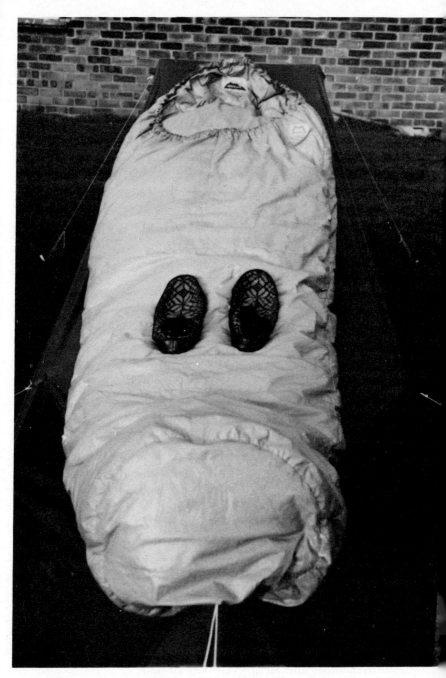

A down-filled sleeping bag and camp slippers

well-constructed, well-designed, tough, all-year-round shelter
at a very reasonable weight and gives good value to the light-
weighter. The tent is available in blue, orange *and green.*

TENT SPECIFICATIONS

	L	W	H	lb	oz
Inner	6′ 8″	3′ 8″	3′ 4″	0	15
Poles			Tapering to rear	0	13
Pegs				0	6
Flysheet				1	9
			TOTAL	3	11

Sleeping Equipment

Now we have got the tent up, we are protected from the rain
and snow, but we are only semi-protected from the temperature. Because of the drop in air and ground temperature at
night, we have to insulate ourselves amply so as to get a full
and uninterrupted night's sleep. To do this we use a lightweight sleeping bag and, if needed, we add highly specialised
bed wear and also we use something to insulate ourselves from
the cold ground.

There is an ample assortment of lightweight sleeping bags
available to the backpacker today. Unfortunately the down
sleeping bag has gone out of favour and is the last choice of
backpackers these days instead of being first choice which it
was only a year or two back. Down was the filling in those
days, but not any more I am afraid for reasons that I have
already explained. It is still, of course, the best choice for a
sleeping bag, with its high insulating qualities and ability to
fold or squeeze into a very low bulk form, but, again, the disadvantage is expense. I don't suppose you can get an all-year-

round down sleeping bag for less than £60 today. Down is best used in conjunction with a sleeping bag liner. Always pack your down sleeping bag into a plastic bag and through doing this it should never become wet. When a down sleeping bag is wet it is useless as far as insulation is concerned; it has to be dry for the down to loft, which is the state of down when at its warmest.

There are different types of down-filled sleeping bags, goose down being the best, then duck, and lastly duck and a feather mixture. The way a sleeping bag is made is a very important factor too. With a badly constructed sleeping bag it is likely that the filling will gather into bundles leaving exposed parts of the sleeping bag vulnerable to severe heat loss. Proper sewn construction stops this and the various types of construction which have been tested for keeping the down in position are listed in order of proficiency starting at the bottom. Firstly there is simple quilting, which is straight sewn lines to keep the down in position. The snag is that heat will be lost through the lines of the stitch. To stop this heat loss, some bags have two simple quilts staggered so the stitch lines are covered by the other bags down, so preventing the loss of heat, this is called double quilting. Then comes wall quilting which also comes in two·types: ordinary box with a straight stitch, with the same problem, and slant wall which eliminates the heat loss again.

Due to down becoming very expensive, other types of material have been slowly taking the market over. The two main other materials or fillings are hollow-fibre fill, which is a polyester-type wadding material, and fibre pile, our good old friend, yes, the same material as in the jackets.

Hollow-fibre fill does not compare with down in the weight for warmth ratio; you need a lot more hollow-fibre fill to get the same degree of warmth that a lower weight of down will achieve. Hollow-fibre fill also does not pack down anywhere near as small as down does, but hollow-fibre fill is a lot cheaper than down and retains its insulative properties even when soaking wet. Mind you, I don't think anybody goes out with the idea of getting their sleeping bag wet anyway.

The pros and cons of fibre-pile sleeping bags are near enough the same as hollow-fibre fill, except that it is probably a bit bulkier still.

Good features in sleeping bags include boxed constructed foots; this construction gives three dimensions of filling layers, so increasing insulation for the feet. Hooded sleeping bags are a must for me. The underside of the bag is cut longer than the top side and shaped round. When drawn up with your sleeping-bag cord it makes a very good hood. This stops the need to wear a woollen hat in bed. When the hood is in action, it is possible just to leave the mouth and nose uncovered and the feel of well-lofted down around your head is enough to make you doze off on its own.

I feel that new backpackers in the future are going to be forced into accepting man-made fillings for their sleeping bags. Excessive prices are now being quoted by retailers for down sleeping bags, simply because they can't afford to have expensive items lying on their shelves, and this is resulting in a cheaper range of man-made fillings for bags. Before long, the words 'down sleeping bag' will be a thing of the past and, when mentioned to new backpackers will have no meaning. There is no doubt that down sleeping bags are the best all-round choice for anybody sleeping outdoors — man-made fibres do not compare; so if you can afford one, get one.

If you do decide on a man-made fibre, the next best to down is probably hollow-fibre fill. It is exactly the same as fibre fill but each fibre is hollowed out to trap more air for insulation.

Night Wear

When backpacking in winter conditions, which includes snow and stiff frosts leading to very low temperatures, unless a very high-grade sleeping bag is being used, you need also a fair bit of insulation next to the skin and filling this need are specialist pyjamas or thermo suits. Also some sort of sock is required to increase heat and comfort whilst sleeping. The best type of bed sock or camp slippers as I call them, are a good pair of woollen socks with a thin plastic under-sole. You can buy this type of sock in climbing shops or easily make them yourself. The beauty about these slippers is as soon as you've pitched your tent, or even before you start to do anything, you can take off your boots and put them on, automatically reviving the feet from the day's travels; when night falls you can use them for bed slippers as well. In the morning if you have to get out of the tent in a hurry you can get straight out of your bag and out of the tent, to relieve whatever needs to be relieved and get back into your sleeping bag, no grovelling and uncomfortable feelings from cold, wet-weather boots. These slippers are worth their weight in fivers and never leave my pack.

Something to Sleep On

To have something to sleep on is more important than one thinks. The earth is not warm and to sleep directly on the ground will result in an uncomfortable night's sleep. There are various ground sheets available which claim to insulate the sleeper from the ground and most of these are very light and with the warmth they bring are worth every ounce they weigh.

First of all I must say I am not keen on air beds; ever since a blow-up hip belt of mine punctured on me I have not been over mad on anything that blows up. Air beds are also cold to sleep on and weigh a bit too much; they are not that comfortable anyway. Polythene ground sheets are not that warm either and are just used to protect the ground sheet really. The all-round best method of ground insulation for the backpacker is a pad made up of closed-cell foam. These pads being foam, weigh hardly anything. They are completely waterproof and don't soak up moisture of any kind. They can be placed under the

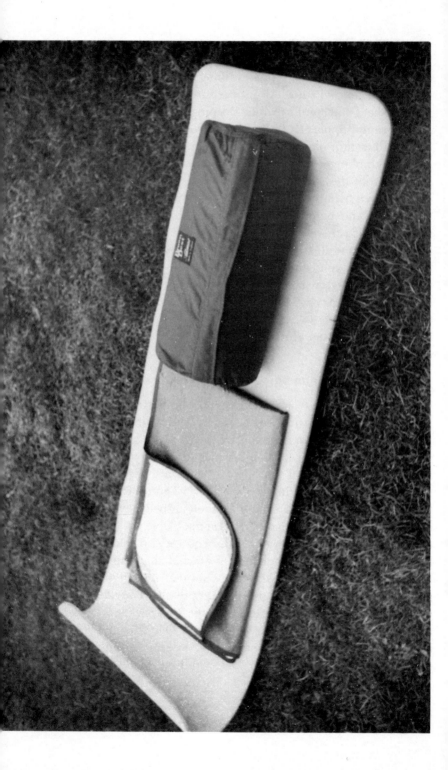

tent's ground sheet to serve both purposes of protecting the ground sheet and insulating the sleeper. They also provide enough bounce to cancel out bumps on a moorland pitch and provide ample comfort for sleeping.

When I really want to be comfortable on a backpacking trip and perhaps need a little more insulation still, because of snow pitching or something like that, I carry the standard thickness mat which is normally about 10mm, and in addition to that I carry a slightly thinner version to cover the whole area of my floor space. This provides real warmth and comfort and the whole set-up still only weighs ounces. Another handy thing to know about ground insulation is that dead bracken, nearly always at hand when on moors or in mountains, is extremely high in insulative properties. I have often spent the night on a bed of bracken; not only was I warm, but to sleep on a bed of bracken is one of the most comfortable feelings to experience. And seeing that the bracken is already there it is silly to pass the chance of gaining comfort without any weight penalty. Scatter the bracken about in the morning though, so the pitch looks exactly as it did when you arrived.

Cooking and Eating Equipment

There is nothing like the open-air life with plenty of exercise for working up a healthy appetite. The backpacker needs an efficient and reliable stove which will work in any conditions. There must be hundreds of different camping stoves being sold in shops all over the country, but only a few are really suitable for backpacking.

In my opinion, the fuels suitable for lightweight camping are gas, meths and petrol. Solid fuel and paraffin have been known to be used, but personally I find them unsatisfactory. Solid fuel hardly produces a flame in still air, let alone on a mountain top, and paraffin, apart from the lack of availability, smells, stains and is generally horrible — I wouldn't even have it near

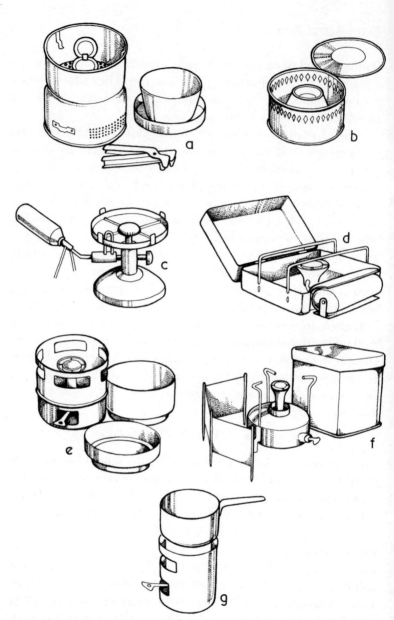

Camping stores: (a) Trangia stormcooker: meths (b) Express Picnic senior size: meths (c) ALP8200 all-weather liquid feed: gas (d) Optimus 8R: petrol (e) Optimus 88: petrol (f) Optimus 90L: paraffin (g) SVEA 123: petrol

my pack, let alone carry it inside.

Availability of fuel isn't a great problem and, in fact, presents no worry on weekend trips, but a little thought is needed if you plan on staying out any longer than four or five days. Gas is quite easy to get hold of and you are bound to find a cartridge somewhere in a village, but the special self-sealable ones are a little bit harder to come across; mind you, two cans should see you through for at least ten days.

Meths can be a devil to find — some chemists stock it and some hardware shops. Mind you, a little meths goes a long way.

Petrol can be bought through two outlets: petrol stations and tobacconists. Don't rely on the latter source though as not all tobacconists sell lighter fuel. If you are really desperate though a kindly motorist and a piece of tubing will solve the problem.

Gas stoves are great; they are efficient, they are very controllable and they are also very hygienic and it is impossible for them to leak. The drawbacks of gas stoves are the weight and the relative lack of heat. They are also temperamental when used in cold conditions. Popular gas stoves include the standard Bluet and the Vango liquid feed. I prefer the latter as the pot stand is spread out at ground level and much more stable than the high-riding Bluet type. There is only one design of meths stove for backpacking, in my view, and that is made by Trangia or Optimus. The two stoves come with their own pots and frying pan.

The stove is made up of two parts of a very light alloy acting as a complete wind shield with a little container for the meths, well protected inside. You can use this design of stove in any wind conditions and it makes no difference to its proficiency at boiling or frying. This is also a very stable stove and would take a mug to knock it over. I've managed to do this on a couple of occasions! But don't worry, that sort of thing only happens to me. The disadvantages with this stove are that the flame is not really controllable, only two levels — low and high — can be

attained and it is also a little bulky when packed.

The best petrol stove available to the lone backpacker today is, in my opinion, the Optimus SVEA 123. This stove has been around a long time and is still very popular. One filling is enough for forty-five minutes of boiling time. It incorporates a smashing wind shield and a reasonably stable pot and pan stand. The only trouble with all petrol stoves is that they have to be primed. This means they have to be warmed up by a little meths or some other fuel burning around the tank to build up enough pressure for the stove to be ignited. This is a little bit annoying at times when only a brew is wanted.

Always plan to have ample fuel and remember, as a rough guide, gas for summer and meths or petrol for winter.

Stoves are also not foolproof, as I find out from time to time, so always treat them with respect and they will function well.

Pots and pans should be light and strong. To be able to cook a full breakfast and evening meal, you really need, as a minimum, an ample-sized frying pan and two pots, so that you can prepare the meal in the one session without washing up a pot in between. A pot grab with holes in (perforated) is a must to round off your billy set and, being perforated, it allows the heat to disperse so that the grab does not become too hot to hold. This little piece of equipment is a lot more important than people think. In fact, you may not come to realise its value until it breaks or is mislaid, but without it frying is difficult and meals can't be taken off the stove until they are cold.

In addition you will need a light plastic plate for eating off and a mug of some sort; in fact, if the mug is enamel you will be able to use it as a pot directly on the stove as well.

Finally, you will need some cut-down cutlery and a good sharp decent-sized lock knife (for safety) — which has many other uses as well. A good refillable lighter is your best method of lighting stoves. Matches are useless when wet, while a lighter will work after being submerged in water. It is also handy if your stove and lighter use the same fuel in case the lighter runs out.

Washing-up kit can be confined to one Brillo pad and a couple of J-cloths, but handfuls of grass will do the job quite efficiently.

3
Equipment for the Trail

When a backpacker goes into the hills for any length of time, he is likely to experience all kinds of weather: gale-force driving rain, hail, snow, frozen temperatures and biting winds — and, his survival in these conditions depends on his equipment.

The four basic pieces of equipment, three of which we have already covered, that the backpacker has to rely on for a comfortable survival are: the tent, which acts directly against the elements, being a waterproof, windproof barrier for the tired and sleeping backpacker; the sleeping bag, which keeps him warm and comfortable at night; a good pair of sturdy boots; and last, but not least, something to take every piece of equipment that is used for the overnight stop, which can weigh anything up to 35lb, and which must be transported. A rucksack or a combination of rucksack and waist pouch is the usual method. It must be as comfortable as possible and, since it is going to be living on your back for roughly a third of the time you are out on a trip, it must be correctly selected for your personal requirements.

Rucksacks

There are only two fundamentally different types of rucksacks available on the market: framed or frameless. The framed

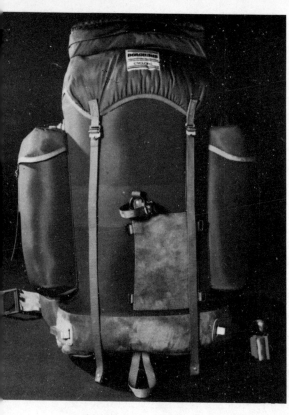

A frameless rucksack

rucksack is used by most backpackers. The combination of frame and sack can be selected to suit the individual and can be bought separately. A sack made by one manufacturer may be paired with a frame made by another. This gives a greater variety of choice for the perfect personal pack and frame.

Framed rucksacks are fine in ideal conditions, on a flat trail, something like the Ridgeway perhaps, where no great amount of climbing is involved and where very strong winds are rare.

When buying your frame, you have a choice of the joints being screwed in or welded. If you can afford it, go for the welded type; they last a lot longer. Most frames are made of aluminium or alloy and these metals are ideal for the purpose.

A mesh backband, an optional extra to a frame, will cut down condensation on the back. These are superbly comfortable and put an end to wet, clammy backs for good. The straps of a rucksack are also a very important consideration: make

A framed rucksack

sure they have enough padding for comfortable travelling and also check that they can be quickly adjusted. You don't want to perform a major operation every time you adjust a strap.

Hip belts, in my opinion, make framed rucksacks worthwhile. If a frame does not have a hip belt, or a waist belt at least, it is not a lot of good for the big-load carrier. A hip belt lies at the bottom of a frame, attached to it by a pin which usually holds the strap connected to the hip belt firmly in that position. When the rucksack is put on to the wearer's back, the hip belt can be lifted and tightened, thus transferring some of the weight that would otherwise rest on the shoulders to the hip. In doing this, it also gives the frame and pack that extra bit of stability when crossing streams or tackling stiles. The hip belt is well worth having and is usually fitted as a standard, but if not try to get one fitted as an extra.

There are moments along the trail when a framed rucksack can be a burden, for example when climbing a stile or a barbed-wire fence (don't ask me what I'm doing climbing a barbed-wire fence — bad route finding!) or crossing a stream using stepping stones. One foot wrong, or a strong gust of wind and you are on the ground, or in the water, which can be nasty with a 35lb pack on your back.

There are no such problems with frameless packs, which hug the wearer's back, acting as part of the wearer. These sacks give the packer much better balance. Climbing stiles becomes enjoyable and easy, rather than a major assault. Frameless rucksacks are made to fit the wearer's back. Some of the better makes have pieces of foam which bend to fit the wearer's back; in that way, all the pack weight is as near to the spine as possible, giving a Rolls Royce ride.

Frameless sacks are also very light indeed. Unloaded they only weigh, on average, half as much as the framed rucksacks, which gives them an advantage to start with. They are also very easy to travel with on public transport. You can squeeze them in a gap anywhere, whereas travelling with a framed rucksack on public transport can be painfully embarrassing in some situations. Lastly, the price of a frameless rucksack is about one half of the price of a framed rucksack.

But there are always snags. It is claimed that frameless sacks cannot carry anything over 25 to 30lb comfortably. I have used a frameless sack with approximately 25lb in it and I must say it was a pleasure to have it on my back. It carried well.

Of course, there are problems. In the summer, as a frameless rucksack hugs your back, you tend to perspire a great deal, especially if you are on an uphill part of the trail. When you stop for a quick brew or a bite to eat, a chill could be caught quite easily with a wet back.

Another problem with frameless rucksacks is the insulating mat attachments. Insulating mats are worth every bit that they weigh to the backpacker. On a framed rucksack, you can easily attach one to the bottom of the frame where there is plenty of room, but with a frameless rucksack the only method you can use is to strap it on the side, which means that you have about eight inches sticking out of one side of your rucksack which is not ideal when walking through trees or bushes.

There are arguments for and against. The most important thing, though, is to choose a rucksack that suits your own requirements. There are always ideal conditions for a design of rucksack. What you have got to do is match your requirements with the ideal sack for your type of travelling.

Another important aspect of rucksacks is how they are packed. Bad packing can mean bad carrying. Basically, all the heavy items should be as high up as possible in the sack. Things like brew-up kit and water should be high up. Your tent and food should be at the top wih your sleeping bag at the bottom for support. If you keep to this method, you should be all right. Another good tip when packing a sack is to put everything in plastic bags. Rucksacks are not always watertight, especially the ones with a lot of pockets attached and if you do get a leaking sack and your sleeping bag gets soaked, you are not going to have a very pleasant night. If you pack your sleeping bag in a thick plastic bag you won't run that risk.

Another method of carrying which can be used either with a pack or on its own for day hikers, is belt pouches. These are attached to a belt which fits round the waist. They are just big enough for items needed on a day hike and put no strain on the hiker as the weight is carried on the hips. Used with a framed rucksack, they can provide the packer with trail snacks without unloading and they also provide convenient storage for a camera or perhaps a monocular. These pouches can also double up as a support for a frameless sack which hasn't a hip belt.

Having decided on the type of rucksack you prefer, think about the colour. If you decide on orange or red, or perhaps yellow, you will be seen from any distance, especially if you are up on open fells. I grant that you will always be safer on the fells if you can be seen, but if you do get into trouble, surely you will have something in your pack that you can wave about? Most sleeping bags these days are made in bright colours. I think that garish colours spoil the scenery and intrude on the natural surroundings.

Just to end this chapter on rucksacks, I would like to talk

about one particular rucksack which has been put on the market by a firm called Karrimor. It looks like a frameless rucksack and carries like one too, but inside the back of the sack is an ordinary frame. I don't know what you would call it, framed or frameless, but it certainly has the advantages of both put together. As I say, it has a proper frame and it also incorporates a true packsack-type hip belt which is far better than the wrap-round waist type of a frameless sack. It is also very stable indeed when carried over mountains or in high winds. The sack is called the Karrimor Jaguar. The sack is designed so that it looks exactly the same no matter how it has been packed; it also carries well whether the lower compartment is empty or packed to the limit.

A Karrimor rucksack with integral frame

It has two main compartments divided into top and bottom, the bottom being opened and closed by a strong double zip. The access to the top, however, is made by a draw cord which is tightened by a cord fastener. The top is intended for sleeping bag and tent storage and is waterproof, while the bottom comfortably holds cooking equipment and food stuffs.

To protect the top compartment of the sack is a large elasticated cover. To tighten the top down and cover the upper equipment you tension two straps which run right down the length of the sack and under the bottom compartment, so as to bring all the weight nearer the wearer's spine which is exactly the right place for comfort. Incidentally, the buckles on the straps are very easy and quick to release and tighten. On top of the elasticated cover is a large zippered pocket which is very handy for a brew kit or a map and compass when not in use along the trail. Two large side pockets are situated in just the right position on the sack and are of ample size for water, fuel, first-aid kit or any other bibs and bobs. A loop and strap are provided to hold an ice axe if working in snow.

This sack is, in my view, the best all-round backpackers' sack available today. It is well made out of strong and robust material and is definitely the most versatile rucksack I have ever worn. The sack retails at about £33 and I have no hesitation in recommending it.

Map and Compass

It is always a good idea to know where you are at all times. But in mountains or on moorlands it is more a matter of life or death because mist can lower the visibility from several miles to a few feet in seconds and it is therefore essential for you to know your location.

Nobody can route-find perfectly, believe me. Tracks are marked on maps that don't exist and new buildings appear. In fact, I will never forget an experience I had with some friends of mine a while ago; one of them had a 2½ in map, and none of us had thought to check the date when it was last revised. Anyway, we had decided to head for a Public House called 'The Leather Bottle' at dinner time as any normal backpacker in his right mind would do. When we arrived at the location which incidentally only had a dirt track leading to it which was suspicious anyway, there was nothing but rubble. Convinced that we had made a route-finding mistake we began to check back the route on the map, just then, a fellow walker appeared around the corner. We explained the whole story. 'The Leather Bottle, you've missed opening time by about twenty-five years', he said. The wretched thing had been demolished years ago and the map was ridiculously out of date.

That's just one of many experiences I have encountered and although funny at the time, it happened in Chiltern country — it could have been far worse in mountain country; in fact, fatal. Wandering about in mist trying to find a track that is not there, then before you can say ooops! you've walked over the edge. It does happen.

The best maps for walkers, climbers and backpackers alike are the 2½ in to 1 mile Ordnance Survey. We are very lucky in this country to have this type of map which shows nearly every little detail of the country: minute dog legs in paths, mountain huts, sheep folds and even walls and fences are shown. Maps like these would be impossible to get in most other countries due to military intelligence laws. The whole of the UK, even minute islands, is covered by these maps and they are available to anyone.

As well as the two-and-a-half-inch, the Ordnance Survey also publish a one-inch-to-the-mile map and these are good for route-finding too, but of course give less detail.

The best type of compass available, in my opinion, is the Silva type. They sell quite a large range, from a basic compass to their élite model, the Ranger 15 TDCL, which has a built-in clinometer to measure angles of hills and a built-in permanent

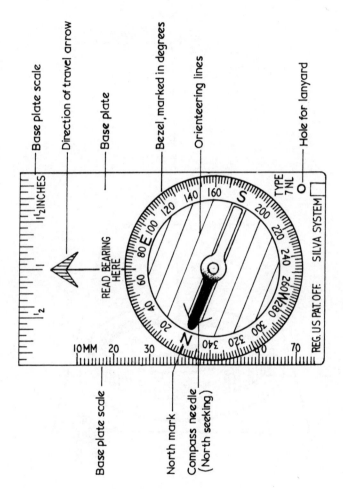

Base plate scale

Direction of travel arrow

Base plate

Bezel, marked in degrees

Orienteering lines

Hole for lanyard

Base plate scale

North mark

Compass needle
(North seeking)

The Silva compass

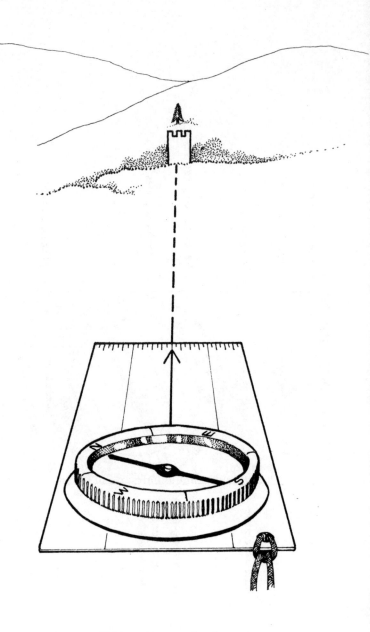

Taking a compass bearing

variation, to save adjustment every time a grid bearing is converted to magnetic. Most of these models have luminous dials which are very handy for walking at night.

I always carry my compass around my neck and slip it into my breast pocket to stop it from knocking. My map is carried in either a proper map case, or in a plastic bag sealed with Blu-tack in my back pocket. The Blu-tack makes it easier to take out and re-fold the map, whereas sellotape tends to rip the bag to pieces.

As far as basic route finding goes, there are only a few points to remember. Never read your compass near anything that might disturb the needle. Make sure you fully understand the National Grid System and are able to give a grid reference. Learn how to rotate your map in conjunction with your compass so that the map is aligned with the ground. Understand how to take a compass bearing from map to ground and vice versa and how to walk on that bearing. Make sure that you know how to read and understand a map and compass. Get used to judging distances and times; learn to read a map in conjunction with the landscape by contours and buildings, etc.

Remember, good route-finding depends on a map, compass and common sense and the ability to use all three together successfully. Lastly, there is no substitute for practice and first-hand experience.

4
Bits and Pieces

The smaller bits and pieces which are needed on a trip are sometimes just as important as the larger pieces of equipment. For an example, let's say your lighter won't work and you've found the flint has worn out and you have left your spare flints at home. Okay, so you have got a spare box of matches sealed from the wet at the bottom of your rucksack somewhere, the problem is solved. No, wait, you have changed your rucksack over to a frameless because of the change in country and you have left your matches at the bottom of your framed sack, which is sitting in your bedroom at home, so you are stuck for a light.

Imagine the trouble it would cause if you were on your own: no hot food or brews. I remember a similar instance; I had arranged a solo trip in the middle of summer to Rome's Latium coast, a sort of a backpacking, hitch-hiking, sun-tan expedition. Well, as you probably know, you are not allowed to take pressurised gas cans on flights, for obvious reasons, so I had to remember to get some gas in Rome before I headed for the coast. I forgot all about it and could not get the right type of can for my stove anywhere on the coast. So I ate cold food all

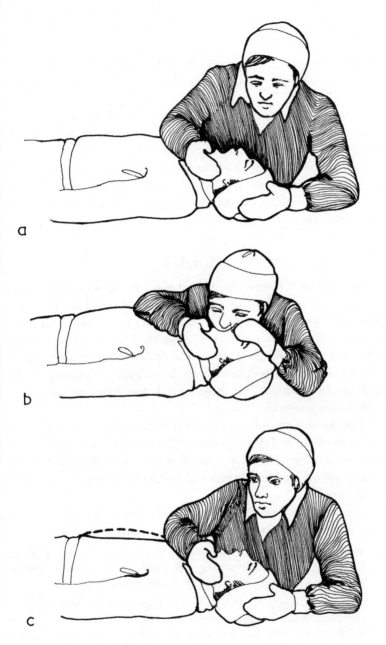

Mouth-to-mouth resuscitation: (a) tilt head back and check that tongue does not obstruct air passage (b) blow into mouth (c) check that chest deflates

through the trip; good job the climate was hot. It might have been much more of a hardship if I had been somewhere like the Alps in winter.

These are just examples pointing out that forgotten bits and pieces, no matter how little they are, can cause an awful lot of trouble. The simple way to eliminate such happenings is to make a checklist of all equipment, no matter how small, that you are ever likely to need on any trip, to anywhere. Then, a quick run down the list before you leave will cut out any possible oversight.

First Aid

A first-aid kit is important, but a basic knowledge of first aid is much more important. A first-aid kit is not much use to you if you don't know how to use it. An easy way of remembering the essential first steps was given to me by a doctor, and I quote from one of his lectures, 'If everybody knew about the "BBC" 75 per cent of the people who die in everyday accidents would still be alive today.' The 'BBC' stands for Breathing, Bleeding and Consciousness.

The knowledge of how to treat serious injuries is easy to learn from the St John's Manual. If you really care for life, you will read it and learn it. Accidents happen not only while backpacking, and so the rules of first aid are equally useful in everyday life.

The 'BBC' makes the lives of people who backpack with you much safer. The basic principles are as follows:

1 When you approach a casualty be calm and collected, but act promptly. Check his breathing; if normal go to 2. If not breathing, give him air by way of mouth-to-mouth resuscitation.

2 Check the whole of the body for haemorrhage (bleeding). If bleeding, stop it by direct pressure on the wound. Do not look for sterilised dressing and waste valuable time in the process; any piece of clothing or even your bare hand will do. Do not take that pressure off at any time.

3 Check consciousness, and note. Turn the casualty into the recovery position and make sure that he is continuing to breath. Stay with the patient.

The recovery position

Just by learning those three stages, you could save dozens of lives. The aims of the first aid are: to sustain life — to stop the condition from becoming worse — to aid recovery.

If you are in any doubt get help as fast as possible but the 'BBC' procedure is far more important than any first-aid kit. Now we have covered that, I will mention the kit.

I must just say that in the years I have been out on trips, I have never had any trouble and the chances of anything happening are very slim. In fact, I will even go as far as to say that an overweight first-aid kit is likely to do more harm than good by weighing down the poor fellow who has to carry it. My own personal first-aid kit contains the following:

  A selection of plasters in different shapes and sizes
  A tube of TCP antiseptic ointment
  A strong metal whistle
  Two safety pins
  A 2p piece

The only important object missing there is a triangular bandage; this can be improvised with clothing, if the need arises. I strongly recommend TCP ointment; it is so versatile you can use it for many things from a wasp sting to a sore bum! Indigestion and pain-killing tablets should also be carried.

The elements, however, are more likely to cause problems than accidents, particularly when out in the hills.

HYPOTHERMIA (exposure)

The cause of exposure is a combination of lack of proper protection from the weather, the weather itself in the form of snow, cold temperatures, hail and wind and, lastly, exhaustion. Exposure occurs when the body cannot cope with the cold; this leads to a rapid drop in temperature in the body's vital organs — hypothermia.

The symptoms are: slowness of physical and mental activity — stumbling, cramp and shivering — slurring of speech — vision impaired — irritability and sudden outbursts — pulse and respiration increase. If any combination of these symptoms occurs, immediately set up camp, or shelter from the weather, and put the patient in a sleeping bag. The priorities are to prevent further body heat loss, to rest the patient, to call for help. Give hot drinks, but no alcohol. All casualties should have medical care, even when they seem to be better.

HEAT EXHAUSTION

If backpacking in summer and excess climbing takes place, heat exhaustion might occur. Causes are over-exposure to ex-

cessive moist heat. Symptoms are: salt loss leading to cramp —
pale cold clammy skin — rapid pulse — fainting — headaches
and dizziness. Treatment: cool the casualty by placing him in
cool surroundings — give him cold water — fan him — seek
medical aid.

FROSTBITE

Frostbite mostly attacks ears, nose, fingers and toes. Symptoms
are: loss of movement — numbness. If not treated immediately, gangrene sets in. Treatment: give the casualty shelter in a
tent and sleeping bag. Warm the affected parts in your hands
and armpits — do not rub or apply direct heat in any way.

CRAMP

The causes of cramp are: excessive body salt lost by sweating
— chilling of the muscles — sudden and too much exercise.
Treatment: stretch the affected muscles — give salt water —
apply deep heat.

Just to sum up then: the ability to prevent accidents, recognise
symptoms and treat them is far more useful than an overweight
first-aid kit.

Lighting

Lighting equipment is hardly necessary in the summer months;
it doesn't get dark before 9.30 pm and is light again early in the
morning, so a mini pen-light is good enough. In fact, if you are
in Scotland in summer time you can forget lighting altogether
as it doesn't really get pitch dark before midnight, and day
breaks again about 4.30am. In autumn though, you might
need a good source of light and I use an Ever Ready mini-light
with special alkaline-powered batteries. These special cells are
made by Ever Ready and Mallory Duracell; they are more ex-

pensive, but give lots more light than the standard type.

In winter, when anything up to twelve hours of darkness can be experienced, then something more substantial and long lasting is needed. Again, the mini-light is enough so long as you don't intend doing any night hiking. For finding a strayed lighter in the inner tent or a lost peg whilst setting up camp, it will serve the purpose. But more substantial lighting is called for when preparing the evening meal, reading a paperback or having the neighbours in for coffee. A candle suits me down to the ground. Either on its own, standing in a container, or fitted in a special candle lantern. A candle on its own is a fire hazard which you should keep in mind if you don't want your expensive lightweight tent to go up in a puff of smoke. You might need a wind shield if you are using a tent which does not have a down-to-earth fly. You can stabilise a bare candle by driving it into the ground.

The candle lantern which I have is hard to come by these days, even in specialist backpacking shops. It is a neat piece of equipment and I love using it. It is made out of very light metal with a glass piece for the light to shine through. It is completely stormproof and has a chain with a hook on the end to hang it from. The warmth that radiates from the top makes a small lightweight tent cosy and, in my view, adds a touch of homeliness to a stormy winter camp.

If you intend to night hike at any point on the trail, or find yourself late arriving at an arranged pitch, a bigger, better torch is needed. All of us have good night vision; given about half an hour in complete darkness to acclimatise, we can see things that we never thought possible. However, after that half an hour, if our eyes are exposed to a bright torch, the night vision is ruined so it is important to use the torch only when absolutely necessary.

Miners' type headlamps have been known to be used by backpackers for night hiking and pitching in the dark, but they have never struck me as being a good idea.

Carrying and Collecting Water

Carrying and collecting water is something that the backpacker has to think about frequently.

I carry my water in a sealable 2 pint polythene bottle, which I find is a good size. In day time I always try to have enough for at least two brews in the bottle. After a brew, fill up again at the next possible watering point. When nearing camp, think about filling up for the overnight stop. The art of this is to fill up as near to camp as possible so as to avoid having to carry it too far. Better still, pitch camp by water if possible. In mountain country, streams are never far away and therefore water need not be carried at all, just brew up or stop for lunch at a stream.

In areas such as the Ridgeway, where water may only be obtainable from the odd cattle trough, it is a good idea to add two purifying tablets to your container to avoid any nasty after-effects.

Try always to boil your water, particularly if it looks suspicious. But I have often drunk water out of puddles; and don't be put off by the colour of mountain streams — it often looks black and sometimes red, which is only due to peat and slack earth formation and, believe it or not, improves the taste.

Personal Gear

My personal bag includes a half flannel and a small piece of soap — anything can act as a towel, but I prefer to carry one in mid-summer in case I decide to go swimming; a comb and mirror — my compass incorporates a mirror so I use that; a toothbrush and half a tube of toothpaste; some tissues (an ample supply, for blowing my nose when I happen to have my waterproofs on) and, of course, for other obvious reasons. That's the washing-kit side of my personal gear, but at weekends I only bother to carry my comb and toothbrush and I don't bother to wash. When the temperatures are down, nobody in their right minds would want a wash anyway. A wash is refreshing at the end of the day or first thing in the morning, but given the choice of having a wash or having a brew, I am afraid the rougher side of my character would win and I would opt for the brew.

My personal gear also includes half a tube of Deep Heat, which I think ought to be standard in every backpacker's kit. It is great for any muscular pains and also acts as a deodorant. I always carry some midge rub in case of an attack and they do attack! I once read somewhere that only three creatures in this world attack without provocation — two were from Africa and the other was the highland midge, so beware!

Odds and Ends

Purifying tablets, some spare matches (sealed from the wet), some spare guy line and guys and four spare pegs, and a spare pair of laces all find a space in my rucksack.

The only reason I take all these odds and ends is that each one can save a weekend from being spoiled.

Plastic bags are very handy for your rubbish, as waterproof containers, as food bags and have a million other uses. A baby tin-opener weighing an ounce ends the list.

Little Luxuries

Little luxuries add to the fun of backpacking and every backpacker carries something that is not strictly essential.

A camera is carried by most backpackers and photographs of past trips put into albums are fun to look at when back at home. Photography is an ideal hobby to go with backpacking.

A monocular is one of my favourite pack friends and can come in useful when wildlife watching, finding a path or even finding a pitch for the night.

If you intend to keep a journal, a notebook and pencil is all you need. Try to be consistent if you intend to keep a log and in years to come it will prove to be great reading, especially in bed on a winter's night.

A paperback book or a guide of some sort can be useful and interesting if you happen to have some time to kill, but remember all these little bits weigh ounces, and ounces weigh pounds, so make sure before you pack them that you are definitely going to use them on the trip.

5
The Wonder Material – Gore-tex

As you may have gathered from the previous chapters, there has always been a problem with water and windproof materials. Not only backpackers, but everyone connected with outdoor activities in the past, has had to put up with condensation and its uncomfortable consequences. Waterproofs and windproofs are completely impermeable to wind and water and that includes body heat and moisture. After walking in waterproofs for any length of time, condensation occurs which dampens the wearer, provoking a chill and causing extreme discomfort.

Until a little while ago, everybody accepted this problem. Then came vague talk about a new material that was supposed to be waterproof and at the same time breathe by letting all the body moisture out through its pores. Gore-tex had arrived.

I must admit that I approached the new materal sceptically. My first assignment was to rigorously test, in every possible condition that arose while backpacking, a Gore-tex weatherproof jacket.

The only weatherproof jacket that was available at that time was the Berghaus and Belstaff jacket. Apart from being Gore-tex material, the Berghaus jacket is extremely well designed with its storm cuffs and hood and tight-welded weatherproof seams. This was the one I obtained. Since then I have tested this garment to the limit, in torrential rain and gale-force winds. It is waterproof and windproof whilst at the same time letting out unwanted moisture and keeping the wearer warm, dry and comfortable. Because Gore-tex laminate, to give it its full title, is functional in this way, it can also be extensively used for low-temperature warm gear, so doing a dual purpose job and also possibly eliminating the need for a duvet or extra sweater. The advantages are staggering. On top of the complete rain suit, which includes jacket, leggings and gaiters, there will in the near future be tents, duvets, sleeping bags and bivvy bags made out of Gore-tex laminate.

Another advantage of the material is that by using a down or fibre-fill sleeping bag with its cover made of Gore-tex, the user gains in insulation for less weight carried and can also bivouac in the summer with full protection from wind and rain.

As with any other new product, the price of Gore-tex is very high, and at the moment only for specialists because of this. Gore-tex will eventually replace other standard outdoor equipment but the price will come down. Gone will be the all-day wet hike in sodden waterproofs and sudden luxury of a warm sleeping bag at night. Life will be easier and better — or will it? I can't help thinking that the sudden interference of modern technology and inventions with backpacking might spoil the simple and traditional lightweight camper's way of life. Is the system, which the backpacker wants to escape from, making outdoor life too easy and comfortable? I have a horrible feeling that the whole idea of making backpacking too simple might just backfire one day. I hope it's after my time! Anyway, Gore-tex is here, and here to stay.

6
Food

Food is a matter of individual preference: whether you are a big eater or a small eater; whether you enjoy eating or not. I personally do not smoke and being generally a fidgety sort, whenever I have time to kill at home, I eat. The meals I eat at home are enormous. Most people eat to live, I live to eat. Some of my best moments while backpacking have been when perched up on some high mountain crag in the snow frying ridiculous midday breakfasts containing gammon steaks, mushrooms, tomatoes, fried slices, kidneys and liver sausage amongst other delightful stodge. This is all great fun but sometimes I overstep the mark. Weight — I mean pack weight — begins to tell and I have to restrict myself to a more modest menu.

When you go backpacking you need ample food, but the right type of food for nutritional value is most important. When choosing food, three guide lines ought to be kept to: firstly, the food that you select must be high in calorific value; there should be no space in the pack for foods that are not good fuels. Walking all day takes a lot out of the body and if you don't get proper nutritious food you are likely to feel tired and cold before the day is out. On average, 4,000 calories per person per day are needed, and more if extreme cold temperatures are experienced. Try to avoid sweating in these conditions, as this is when your body is burning too much fuel at once. The second pointer to keep in mind is the weight in relation to calorific value. Try to keep the weight down as much as possible while still retaining the calories. And lastly, do as much planning and preparation as possible at home, so as to cut the cooking time down to a minimum when actually on the trail. It is no fun having to spend half an hour cooking when you have covered about 20 miles, but don't be tempted to skimp on food and go to bed on an empty stomach. This is wrong and the consequences will be felt next day when the first hill is encountered.

There are some foods that the backpacker simply cannot cope with. Personally, I have nothing to do with eggs. Carried as they are, or broken and stored in a polythene bottle, both spells disaster to me. If you do carry them as they are, they are liable to crack and cause all sorts of trouble in the pack and even when transported in a bottle leakage is a worry. They are not easy or quick to cook either: boiling them is definitely out because of precious fuel and water loss and I always seem to leave half the egg on the pan when I fry them. Dried egg is a different matter though.

Lots of people swear by bread substitute and here is one who swears at it! A while ago the in-thing amongst backpackers was to take the Ryvita-type crispbread and tube cream cheese instead of good old bread and butter. There is no taste in crispbread, it crumbles easily and anyway I used to get the tube of cheese mixed up with my toothpaste! No, seriously, a thick piece of brown bread and butter with a hunk of cheese and a hot brew of soup does a lot more for the backpacker. I realise bread weighs a fair bit and is bulky but I prefer it to any crispbread.

The first thing I do in the morning is to brew either coffee or tea and with this delightful cuppa I have a wheatmeal biscuit — the old services type. This is the first stage. Then comes the full backpacker's fry-up, including anything from bacon, sausages,

A suitable pitch for the night can be difficult to find in farmland *(above)* but open moorland *(below)* will provide plenty of good sites.

kidneys, liver sausage, tomatoes and mushrooms, to anything else I may have to throw in. All these ingredients contribute to a good healthy day on the path. Round that off with a thick slice of bread and butter and a final brew.

Snacks can be useful from then on and chocolate bars, muesli, biscuits, chocolate fudge, chocolate peanuts and raisins all keep the wolf from the door. The first one or two nights out are the occasions to get rid of all your major weight and evening meals can be built around a pork chop or a 'double-sized boil-in-the-bag', finished off with some instant potato or a bag of crisps. To finish the meal, some dried apple flakes with custard or even the odd fresh apple, then some chocolate and a coffee and it's good night from him!

If you intend staying out in wild mountain or moorland areas for long periods and stocking-up points are limited, then you cannot possibly carry the type of food I have just been talking about. Three or four days worth of that type of food weighs far too much. Enter dried foods especially designed for us mountain goers. Lately the backpacker has been blessed with a new type of dried food which only needs boiling water poured on to it and then five minutes for hydration. You can eat it straight from the bag, saving any washing up. This type of food is available from Springlow and Raven Foods.

These dried meals are ideal on long hostile mountain trips, as water in these areas is easy to come by. The art of eating when backpacking is to take enough, but not too much. This is hard to gauge and takes a few trips before you can get it right. Remember, though, eating is an important part of a trip, but can also become a burden. The happy medium is the answer, and only trial and error will lead to it.

7
Backpacking Country

Wherever you live in the United Kingdom, backpacking country is not far away. It might be those few green bits a couple of miles out of town, or that group of mild hills with a trig point on top in the corner of the Ordnance Survey map. There is always somewhere easily accessible and each area has its own individual character. Backpackers tend to like their own local country. Here new tents can be tested and new gear tried out and, in particular, boots can be broken in.

My local area is the Chiltern Hills. I am very fond of them and have discovered many wild woodland pitches over the years. I have often received telephone messages like: 'Meet you at 205 176 tonight!' A quick rucksack pack, a discreet raid on the larder, a brisk motor to the nearest path leading to that grid reference, then a grovel about in a wood in pitch dark, while at the same time wondering where the hell I am until suddenly spotting a vague tent shape flickering in the light of a candle lantern. You give a couple of flashes of your torch, a reply — great, it's your friend. You proceed and your arrival is greeted by a hot brew and a perfect, level pitch selected for you.

I have done this many times and it is how a local 'overnighter' ought to be. Nobody knows you are there, nobody can see you or hear you, so it doesn't matter — you are not doing anything wrong. But as soon as somebody sees you, watch out!

You are suddenly trespassing, and polluting the countryside, and making a nuisance of yourselves. So, the answer is, don't be seen — be discreet. Never do any harm to the countryside in any way, and always clean your rubbish up after you. This is backpacking at its best — but always abide by the Country Code.

We are lucky in this country to have such a vast footpath network. Most of the tracks were once main roads many years back and make great paths for walking on. Wherever you are, the Ordnance Survey map will mark a path close by. Best backpacking country includes forests, where wild-life predominates, especially deer; and coasts, where walking can be really rewarding and the bird-life plentiful. Appetites flourish on the coast — what with the sea air and the up-down-in-out walking. Gentle hill country, which is mainly found in the South and includes the Cotswolds, the Chilterns and the Downs, is the kind of country which is great for the beginner. Moorland is most certainly backpacker's country, and the need for proper use of map, compass and brain is essential. The wind howls and snow can fall without warning, so be prepared for the worst. The élite backpacker's country is mountain ranges. Down south is, I'm afraid, sadly lacking in them. The best mountain ranges are to be found in Wales, the Lake District and Scotland. Special care and attention to equipment and personal experience is necessary, though, and if you plan to visit these areas in mid-winter it is advisable to carry crampons and an ice-axe.

Long-distance paths, especially those comprising existing paths to form one long, marked trail, are great for backpackers who prefer to aim for a destination rather than wander aimlessly about. The first official long-distance path was the one and only Pennine Way — the path backpackers love to hate. It runs almost the entire length of the Pennine chain and over the Scottish border into the wild and woolly Cheviot Hills. The whole path is 250 miles long, and includes some of the most beautiful parts of Britain, but, I also hasten to add, some of the most inhospitable parts, too. I have done the path once and exactly half of it on another occasion. In my opinion, you need at least three weeks to enjoy the route, which allows a little time over for a rest day or two when it is pouring down. Personally I think it is a great path. It has been described as the M1 of walking, but anyone out on Kinder Scout or Great Shunner Fell on a winter's afternoon might conclude that the walker's M62 would be a more suitable nickname.

National Parks are great areas for backpacking — mostly moorland or mountain regions. These are my favourite areas, for they are particularly beautiful and wild. We have ten altogether: the Lake District, the North York Moors, the Peak District, Snowdonia, Brecon Beacons, the Pembroke Coast, the Yorkshire Dales, Exmoor and Dartmoor. They are designated National Parks to protect these beautiful areas of our national heritage against development or new building. The National Parks are controlled by the Countryside Commission, and each National Park has a local administrative authority in control. In fact, they are also responsible for any factors which may influence the appearance of the countryside within the National Park in any way.

Other areas which are not quite big enough or as spectacular as the National Parks are designated by the Countryside Commission as 'areas of outstanding natural beauty'. These include my own lovely Chiltern Hills, the Cotswolds, the Downs, Bodmin Moor and the Forest of Bowland, amongst many others. All the long-distance footpaths, National Parks and areas of beauty are just beckoning to be walked on, so off you go. Yes, next weekend will do!

Wild Pitches

I must stress that these four pitches are wild and miles away from the nearest habitation. Permission to pitch on any wild site must be sought first from the owner. This is very important if the good name of backpacking is to flourish.

Map identification — 6-figure grid reference

OS Ben Nevis and Glen Coe Tourist Map,
one inch to the mile   222 638

OS Lake District Tourist Map,
one inch to the mile   318 095

OS Peak District Tourist Map,
one inch to the mile   083 904

OS Dartmoor Tourist Map,
one inch to the mile   636 656

First Night Camp Site Bases

Most of these bases are ideal for a heading point in the evening, so that you know that you are going to have somewhere to pitch and leave the car for the first night. When you travel to your destination at a weekend, it will probably be on a Friday night, and if in winter, it will certainly be dark when you arrive, so a camp-site is very handy. There are many farm sites in valleys and these are within ideal striking distance of mountains and moorland.

Such sites are marked on OS Tourist Maps and are available in directory form in many site guides. These useful guides are to be found in most bookshops.

The Country Code

Guard against all risk of fire
Fasten all gates
Keep dogs under proper control
Keep to the paths across farm land
Avoid damaging fences, hedges and walls

Leave no litter
Safeguard water supplies
Protect wild life, wild plants and trees
Go carefully on country roads
Respect the life of the countryside

International Distress Signal

6 blasts of a whistle or 6 flashes of a torch in 1 minute.
Answer with 3 blasts or 3 flashes.

Areas of Outstanding Natural Beauty and National Parks in England and Wales, and Long-distance Footpaths

Areas of outstanding natural beauty	Area in sq km	Area in sq miles
Gower	189	73
Quantock Hill	99	38
Lleyn	155	60
Surrey Hills	414	160
Dorset	1,036	400
Northumberland Coast	129	50
Cannock Chase	68	26
Shropshire Hills	777	300
Malvern Hills	104	40
Cornwall	932	360
North Devon	171	66
South Devon	332	128
East Hampshire	391	151
East Devon	267	103
Forest of Bowland	803	310
Isle of Wight	189	73
Chichester Harbour	75	29
Chilterns	800	309
Solway Coast	107	41
Sussex Downs	1,507	582
Anglesey	215	83
South Hampshire Coast	78	30
Norfolk Coast	450	174
Kent Downs	845	326
Suffolk Coast and Heaths	391	151
Dedham Vale	57	22
Wye Valley	325	125
North Wessex Downs	1,738	671
Mendip Hills	202	78
Arnside and Silverdale	75	29
Lincolnshire Wolds	560	216
Total	14,462	5,583

National Parks in England and Wales	Area in sq miles
Lake District	866
Snowdonia	845
Yorkshire Dales	680
North Yorkshire Moors	553
Peak District	542
Brecon Beacons	519
Northumberland	398
Dartmoor	365
Exmoor	265
Pembrokeshire Coast	225

Long-distance footpaths	Length in miles
Pennine Way	250
Offa's Dyke Path	168
Pembrokeshire Coast Path	167
North Downs Way	141
North Cornwall Coast Path	135
South Cornwall Coast Path	133
Cleveland Way	93
South Devon Coast Path	93
Ridgeway Path	85
Somerset and North Devon Coast Path	82
South Downs Way	80
Dorset Coast Path	72

Some of the best backpacking areas

Long-distance Footpath Guide

Long-distance footpath	Start	Finish	Good pitching ability (0-10)	Water access (0-10)	Route-finding	Type of terrain
Pennine Way	Edale	Kirk Yetholm	9	9	No comment—but take your Wainwright	Mainly moorland
Cleveland Way	Scarborough	Helmsley	7	8	Average	Moorland and coast
Pembrokeshire Coast Path	St Dogmaels	Amroth	6	6	Dodgy when path leaves coast	Much wildlife and remote coastline
Offa's Dyke Path	Chepstow	Prestatyn	8	7	Be alert all the time — many stiles	Varied moorland, forest and rolling foothill country
South Downs Way	Harting	Eastbourne	6	6	Some bridleways; fair	Gentle hill country
North Downs Way	Farnham	Dover	5	6	Fairly easy	Gentle hill country
Ridgeway Path	Overton Down	Ivinghoe Beacon	6	5	Easy to start with, becoming difficult	A mixture of downs and delightful, wooded hills
South-West Peninsula Coastal	Minehead	Studland	6	6	Just follow the coast	Varied coastline

8
Backpacking Technique

Whether it is your first trip, or your hundred-and-first trip, remember, you are out to enjoy yourself and that is the main aim. Try and slow down a bit and not worry too much about the distance covered in miles.

I remember one of my first trips was on the Upper Ridgeway; I was backpacking on my own and that particular night I camped high up on a Down in a copse of trees. All evening, I was planning on how many miles I could 'knock up' before dinner time the next day. Anyway, I had planned to get to the small Chiltern town, Princes Risborough, by dinner. Come first light, having eaten my breakfast, I was ready to pack up and go. I was on the Ridgeway by 5.30am and already in overdrive. I was really pushing it; and come ten o'clock I needed my first proper rest. I brewed up and slumped pathetically against a tree. I was very tired, and so early on in the day. I couldn't understand it. I packed up and started to walk again, not surprisingly with great difficulty. Soon I needed another rest and another rest — I was finding the going hard and as the sun began to reach its hottest at midday, I was wondering if I would ever reach Risborough — I could hardly walk.

Ever since that day, I have never rushed off early on in the morning and have always paced myself during the day, pre-planning stops and brews and conserving energy. Remember, you don't have to prove yourself to anybody but yourself, so there's no need to trail blaze, just relax and enjoy yourself.

Planning and Packing

Having got all your kit together, which includes clothing, boots, rucksack and its contents, all that is left is to pack up and go. The tiny spark which ignites the passion to go backpacking can be caused by a number of events. As you pull into the firm's car-park you notice that all the spaces have gone, you're late as it is. Just as you are backing in, a lorry blocks your way. You eventually arrive and proceed to the cloakroom, having the misfortune to pass the Boss on the way. 'Morning Sir!', 'Afternoon, Peters' he says, looking at his watch in a sarcastic, sickening sort of way. You tell him to Harvey Smith off under your breath. Good! Good! The spark is slowly igniting.

Later on in the week, the firm's groveller walks in just as you are making a private long-distance phone call. It's no good, he has overheard you and knows it is not a business call. You are summoned before the boss for a right royal roasting. 'I didn't get where I am today by using the Company's telephone'. 'Go and jump in the lake.' 'What was that?' 'Nothing Sir.' And so on.

Friday eventually arrives and you are literally smoking with pressure. Following four telephone calls for orders, six Tannoy calls and a couple of awkward customers, you are just about to tear your hair out. The work is piling up and the boss telephones to tell you to get your finger out. The eruption occurs; a fist is buried into a nearby hardboard wall. You decide backpacking is the answer.

Plan your meals ahead with fuel, value, practicability and personal preference in mind. Pack all your food in plastic bags for freshness and for protection from rain and possible spillage.

Check through your personal checklist. Sleeping bag, stove, tent? What about your boots? So the time of departure arrives after all the careful planning.

You are packed, amply clothed for the worst weather that might occur and all ready to go. Money in pockets, identification by YHA membership card. You have decided on the location and where you will start from, but how do you get there?

The most practical method is by car, but not everybody has one. Other choices are train, National Bus or hitch-hiking. Obviously car is the most economical way of transport, excluding hitch-hiking, of course. The advantages of a car are that you can go and come back at whatever time you wish and you can also get to the remotest village and mountain areas where the train cannot. There is the constant worry though of leaving your car un-attended. There is also the pressure of driving to your destination on a Friday night, especially if the starting point is a considerable distance away. I personally hate driving long distances and opt for the train if there is a station near where I want to start from. To my mind, it is the only really comfortable way to travel. Rail transport is very expensive though, especially at weekends, but if you can travel mid-week, then considerable savings can be made.

National Bus travel is reasonable for the very modest price they charge and these express coaches will get you to mountain villages. If you have time on your hands and limited funds, then hitch-hiking is the only answer. Just remember, though, that lifts don't come that easy and time on the trail can be lost in getting there. Just use common sense and look tidy and happy and a lift will come along sooner or later.

Four or five years back at Christmas time a friend and I planned a complete Ridgeway assault. Arriving at Overton Hill late on Christmas Eve by means of train and taxi, we hurriedly walked a few hundred yards up the way and pitched our tents, so we could get down the pub for a quick one before closing time. This we did and, on the way back, noticed how clear the sky was with its sparkling stars. We commented that it should be a good day tomorrow whilst climbing into our nylon shelters and cocoon-like sleeping bags.

Came the morning with loud gusts of wind and torrential rain, and my friend's tent was slowly falling down to top it all. Now, I don't know if anybody has been at Overton Hill in these conditions on a Christmas morning, but it was pretty morale flagging. Lying in our sleeping bags, we began to think of turkey, mince pies, Christmas pud, booze, paper hats and Laurel and Hardy. The weather was just not going to get better so we decided to go home, but how, on Christmas Day? We began to walk towards Marlborough on the A4 sticking our thumbs out half-heartedly. A few juggernauts and an hour went by before a little orange Fiat approached and actually stopped. Before I had realised my luck I had been dropped off about half a mile from where I live. As I arrived home, my family was just preparing Christmas dinner. A quick change and wash and I made it to the table just in time, as if I hadn't been away at all. Ever since then, I have given Christmas a miss for backpacking. It's as if something is telling you that it is not quite right to be out on Christmas Day.

Your method of getting to your starting point will determine to some extent the planning of your route. The choice is either to go straight from A to B or a circular walk arriving back at your starting point. If you can walk to a railway station then great — A to B it is, but if you have left your car where you started, then you either have to walk back to it or get transport back to your car from B. Remember too, you are not going to find an efficient commuter service in the middle of the Lake District, but you may get a ride with the school bus.

Okay, so transport has been sorted out. You arrive raring to go. If it is your first time backpacking, you will be anxious to get started, you will have butterflies and start to doubt your equipment, and yourself. What happens if the mist comes down? etc. Don't worry, in no time you will be striding along without a worry in the world. Old timers will know what it is all about and will walk confidently and steadily. Right then, out of that café and off we go. Just for convenience, let's say we are about to backpack into a moorland, mountain area.

Travelling

Although in a sense we have only got to our starting point, I would like to talk about travelling as if we had already been out a couple of days. So at the moment we have packed our tents away and are ready for the next day's walking.

It is always worth having a little session before actually walking, to discuss where you intend to walk. Get the maps out and plan a rough route, leaving ample time for brews and rests. Also take the weather situation into account. You might have heard a bad weather forecast for your area on your mini-radio the night before so it might be best to skip the 3,000ft mountain that you had included in your route. Plan roughly where you intend to pitch and generally try to stick to what you plan. Map case round the neck, compass at hand, belt pouch in position with camera and travelling snacks inside. Now shoulder up your pack, get comfortable, grab your walking stick or ice axe, one quick look around the pitch to make sure you have not forgotten anything and tally-ho! We're off.

One of the hitches you might experience, especially if you are new to backpacking, is blisters. Luckily, I have never had a blister in my life — touch wood. I am told blisters are caused by ill-fitting boots and rough socks. With every stride the creased sock rubs in the same spot all the time until a blister is formed and the continual rubbing of the sore cripples the sufferer — no longer can he enjoy his travelling. The best way to prevent this from happening is to make sure your boots and socks are correctly fitting. At any stops take the opportunity of taking your boots off. Even a paddle in a nearby stream can make the feet ready for the next stage.

Treatment can be Dr Scholl's Moleskin stuck well over the blistered area.

There must be a reason why I have never had any trouble with blisters, and toughening up the skin may have something to do with it. I have had football boots, training shoes and riding boots on at different intervals since I have started backpacking, so perhaps these have hardened up my skin. Always start off steady and keep the pace to a minimum; don't worry about miles covered and don't tear along like a US Cavalry charge, then gradually unbutton the top garment to help ventilation. At the first tinge of hunger, I dig into a travel snack. After half an hour I have a stop for five minutes. I honestly believe that you can cover more miles by stopping every hour for five minutes and, in fact, more frequently if you feel tired. After about three hours, the big stodgy breakfast will wear off — this is a signal for the first proper brew up of the day.

I always get out my tent ground sheet or a piece of close-cut foam to sit on. This piece of equipment is known as the the 'sitzmat' between backpackers. It enables you to sit in comfort, dry and warm instead of getting a wet backside. Sometimes a large flat stone suffices.

Ah, the brew, the brew. The backpacker's revival system; there's nothing quite like a brew to raise flagging spirits and I find I can press on quite happily after an already long day's mileage after a hot brew. I opt for a hot brew in mid-summer as it seems to put something back into the travel-tired backpacker, and more so than a cool soft drink. After the water has boiled and the brew made, I fry some bacon and have a bacon butty. I swear by bacon butties and reckon on about 5 miles to one and a brew. As I personally use my frying pan quite a lot in a day's backpacking, what with breakfast and midday feasts, I find that it is better to wash my frying pan only once every three or four days. I also keep the same fat in the pan by allowing it to harden at the end of every fry. The advantage of this is that it

saves weight, because by not throwing away the fat every time
you have a fry, the spare fat carried is kept to a minimum. All
you need is ample fat in your pan and a bit spare to cover you
for eight days. Another advantage is that the frying pan is
immediately ready for use; but carry a special bag to keep your
pan in, so preventing staining other gear in the rucksack.

After three or four days on the trail, you will begin to get in
the rhythm of things and will start to lose the stiffness and feel
fit. Walking will become an almost effortless pleasure and this
is when the joy of backpacking begins.

The combination of knowing you can rely on your equipment, the confidence in your route-finding ability and your
effortless walking momentum will all contribute to the enjoyment experienced. Walking, however, is not always effortless;
some days you will not seem to be able to get going and yet
other days will cover 25 miles without a thought. In the middle
of the walking day, sudden energy bursts occur. These strange
experiences are hard to explain. You just feel in your limbs that
you have to go.

When it starts to rain on the trail, make sure that it is going
to continue before you put your waterproofs on. To cut down
condensation inside the waterproofs, slow down the pace of
your walk, so slowing down sweating. When the rains are
mean and really wetting, the temptation to miss out brews and
stops is strong. Nobody really wants to stop in weather like that
and all that is on the mind is the night's pitch and that glorious
sleeping bag. It's okay to press on and get there, but remember
you must eat, to keep going and to give you warmth, and for a
morale boost. These restrictions of stops, food and rest all lead
to exhaustion and a lowering in body temperature which leads
directly to exposure. Walking in that sort of rain isn't much fun
and I for one don't pretend to enjoy it. If the day looks really
bad and the rain really mean, I often stay inside my tent and
sleeping bag for the day and rest up with a continuing flow of
brews, dozes and 'jimmy riddles'! Don't ever let the weather

upset you — just be philosophical about it.

Walking in snow is a different kettle of fish. A whole new world waits to be explored. In these conditions, it is relatively easy for the hiker to keep warm, except perhaps for the feet (stamping remedies this). Dangers in walking on the snow do exist; a slip near the edge of a cliff could end in tragedy, but sure footing and an ice-axe reduces the risk.

You may come across almost anything while backpacking. A friend of mine, while solo backpacking in the New Forest, got lost among the many tracks that confuse backpackers. While wandering about trying to find his bearings a nude woman pranced across his path. Closer observation revealed a whole family with no clothes on. Apparently this family were very keen on nudism and did this every weekend through the summer. So, if you are interested just go ahead — let it all hang out backpackers! I often come across odd bits of aircraft and under-carriages whilst out backpacking. All these unusual happenings go on and add to the joy of the trail. There are more natural things to see though, like historic buildings and old mine shafts, which are great to explore so long as you are looking where you are going.

In the mountains, paths are way-marked by cairns, with usually an extra large cairn on the summits. These are built by walkers and the convention is to add a stone to the stack to ensure that the cairn stays as large, if not larger, so everyone can be guided in mist.

Refuge huts are to be found in mountains too, especially in Scotland where they are called bothies. These huts are either transported up there by helicopter or tractor and put in positions where they are likely to be needed most, or are simply modified shepherd huts. Most of the huts are open to anybody who cares to use them, but simple rules like leaving some food, usually dried, have to be obeyed so as to keep them well-stocked up for emergencies. In addition to food, there is usually a stove, a first-aid kit, something to sleep on and an emergency

A good pitch

blanket. These huts are great to spend the night in, especially if
the weather is really wicked outside, and if you're lucky you
might stumble across one of the few that have fireplaces.

Camping

Basically you can pitch where you want and this particularly
applies when in open moorland and mountains. Legally,
though, you must seek permission; if you don't, the owner is
quite within his rights to turn you off at any time during the
night. You must look for pitches and develop an eye for them;
the beginner tends to look for something looking like a golfing
green. Perfect pitches do not always appear like magic —
improvise.

Your pitch should be on a reasonably flat surface, but if it
does slope make sure your head is uphill. Check the surface for
any large bumps that might ruin a night's sleep and make sure
it is clear of any foreign objects like animal excretion, twigs,
etc.

Always look for a piece of flat ground around the front of the
pitch to stand the stove on. Stream pitches are great and the
sound of water rushing by your tent is enough to send you off to
sleep, also unlimited water is available for drinks and washing
— 'Five Star Accommodation'!

Protection from wind ought to be considered and in mountains it is just as well to let walls, bracken, land structure,
banks and shepherd huts take the full force rather than your
little lightweight tent. However, if you are caught in a strong
wind, it might be a good idea to check the pegs and guy lines if
you happen to wake up in the middle of the night. It does take a
fair bit of wind to blow down a properly erected tent, though,
so don't worry too much.

Avoid pitching in hollows where the rain might cascade over
you and choose ground which is well drained. Also avoid
pitching near animals. Cows are attracted to a strange, small,

lightweight tent. It is not as if they intend to do any harm, they are just born nosy and clumsy. Cows don't trip over guy lines — which is just as well, otherwise there would be a lot of squashed backpackers around — they crash through them.

Horses are comedians, are a hell of a lot cleverer than people think and are also very playful. Wild ponies are nothing to bother about and will ignore you, but if you ever pitch in a field with a friendly pony, watch out. It is advisable not to leave your tent alone with the pony while you stomp up to the pub for the evening because when you get back there very well might not be any tent at all! Ponies won't hurt you, but are practical jokers with sometimes warped senses of humour.

When in farmland, never pitch anywhere near a bull. You are not dealing with playful ponies or nosy heifers any more, but a few tons of angry roast beef. No, seriously, I can't emphasise enough the dangers of bulls when camping, or walking for that matter. When I meet one on the trail, I don't pretend to be anything less than terrified and, remember, there is reason to be terrified too. I have heard various theories about the best method of dealing with a charging bull — none of them would I trust for a second. The best way to deal with a bull in a field is to go round that field, but if you must cross it then cause as little rumpus as possible and pass through as quickly and as discreetly as you can while keeping an eye on him at all times.

When pitching in mountains or moorland, the only animals that will be around are sheep and unless a special killer breed exists that I know nothing about, you are quite safe!

When you are walking through the day, always keep a sharp eye open for pitches that might come in useful on other occasions. I have so many of these pitches in my head now that I have gathered over the years that all I need to do is to pick up a map of a backpacking area and dozens of pitches start flooding back that I have seen or pitched on at one time or another. If you fancy recording these sites, the best way to do it is by grid references. You can take it further and photograph them. Also grading them by personal preference would make an interesting pitch directory.

When you eventually do find a suitable tent site, have a quick look at it before you start to erect your tent. It is as it should look when you have packed up and gone — exactly the same as you found it — unless there was some litter about when you arrived in which case you should tidy that up before you leave.

The position in which your tent should be faced is mainly governed by which way the wind is blowing and, of course, the slope of the ground. Lots of backpackers swear by pitching in a certain direction so as to catch the sun on the back of their tents in the morning. I personally don't think this is very practical. When pitching in mountains it is best to try and pitch with the tail of the tent into the wind, but when the wind blows in rough country, it comes from all directions, so it doesn't make that much difference. The priorities in positioning my tent on a pitch go like this: Firstly I consider the slope — if there is one there, I like to face uphill; then I position my tent towards the best view while still considering the direction of the wind.

Pitch the fly first, if possible, in case there's a sudden downpour and, when pegging out, angle the pegs at least 45°. Make sure all guy lines and peg points are secure and tight. When in mountains, due to the sometimes strong winds, it is advisable to cross-peg the guy points and place stones on these pegs to ensure they don't pop out in the night.

Now we have got our shelter all secured from nasty happenings, we can start the evening's activities by unpacking the gear needed for the stop. Get out your sleeping bag and give it a nice airing by turning it inside out and putting it somewhere where it will be safe and also catch a breeze.

Assemble your stove and cooking gear and put your lighter and fuel at hand. Get those boots off if you have got comfortable camp footwear and then get down to the nitty-gritty of brewing, and cooking the evening meal. The first step I take when preparing this meal is to get organised; I sort myself out by having everything at hand for the meal so I don't have to get up for anything. If it is raining, the cooking must take place under the flysheet, but if the weather is fine, I am a great believer in cooking outside. From now on try to adopt a leisurely attitude. Take time over everything. This is the time to get rid of those inner-city tensions.

When you start to cook your meal, make sure the stove is stable and no nasty accidents can happen. I have been known to hurtle stoves into the night from my tent, because of spillage from the stove. In fact, I am quite famous for having accidents with stoves. Once a Gaz stove pipe snapped whilst I was cooking a pan full of sausages, the naked pipe and shooting flame turned on my leg, nearly burning me severely. With that, I hurtled the lot away from the tent, including the sausages — which were ruined!

After the meal has been eaten (straight from the pan or pot that you cooked it in so avoiding washing plates up) you can mumble to yourself modestly, 'that was a superbly cooked meal, Peters, I wouldn't mind another dollop of that', and let the washing up of your pot or pan wait until the inclination takes you. Boiling water with a Brillo pad or tussock of grass will do the job amply. In fact, a hunk of moorland grass with its roots used as a scourer makes a superb dish washer if fuel is low, or you just feel too downright idle to put on a pan to boil.

I hope you didn't rush your evening meal because if you did a stomach-ache will start shortly. I'm a great one to talk; I am afraid I am a natural bolter of food and experience these stomach-aches regularly. An indigestion tablet is usually the answer and, after a short time, 'gannet Peters' is himself again.

After a little doze perhaps, discuss what you are going to do for the evening with your companions. Perhaps you fancy a pub for the evening. Have a look on the map to see if one is nearby. Okay, we are going down to the pub are we? Don't forget your waterproofs then and make sure you haven't left anything outside of the tent; zip the door up, hide valuables and off we go.

Country pubs are really friendly places and if you offer the landlord a drink you will leave a friendly impression of hikers in general in his mind. You will also very probably get an account of the history and goings on in the area. Log fires are a common nuisance in country pubs because once you get near them you don't want to go back to the pitch at closing time, especially if it is doing something outside, so try and ignore the initial temptation. Don't be frightened about getting a little bit 'tipsy' — it will help you get to sleep.

Of course, there are other activities to be enjoyed in the evening. If you are pitched wild, why not have a fire? By a fire, I don't mean a furnace; a little fire big enough for all to sit round is ample. Fires lend themselves to sing-songs and brews, and what could be pleasanter than good companionship around an open log fire without a care in the world? Old Baden-Powell wasn't such a bad fellow was he? After chatting well into the night, you bid your companions sweet dreams — the chatter will commence again when all have retired to their little mountain homes.

A final check on the peg points, into the sleeping bags, then light the candle lantern and have a final night-cap. After more chatter you slowly doze off to sleep, tired from the day's travels. I personally have some snacks and a brew ready in case I wake up hungry or thirsty, but this is only personal.

You may well be woken up in the middle of the night by strange noises, these sounds usually have sensible explanations so don't sit up all night terrified. I have certainly been through this type of situation before, but now I would even invite Frankenstein in my tent for a brew and a game of crib without blinking an eyelid! When you have had Land-Rovers belting towards your tent in the middle of the night and have sighted possible UFOs you don't worry too much about odd noises. Do try to get a good night's sleep though, as rest is a very important aspect of backpacking if a good enjoyable day on the trail is to be had.

When I awaken in the morning, which is normally at first light, the very first thing I do is to put the brew on, the first cuppa of the day is always the best and I enjoy it immensely with an oatmeal biscuit while still in my sleeping bag.

I delay going to the loo in the morning as long as I can if it is tipping down and sometimes peep outside my tent thinking that at least the alternative would be warmer!

Talking about the loo, do burn your paper, and remember to kick a small hole before you go, then to cover it up again with soil or a large boulder. Always make your loo where it is very unlikely that people will wander, somewhere way off the path.

After you have relieved yourself and had the first brew, the full breakfast can be cooked, whilst still in the sleeping bag. Again, get organised and have everything to hand. When frying, watch the spitting fat and open the fly sheet to prevent it getting stained. If you are lucky, the odd mushroom may be picked and put straight in the pan. Breakfast is a glorious meal and sometimes I have two panfuls, the smell of bacon really gives me an appetite when camping.

Breaking camp can be done fairly easily when the weather is nice. Put your sleeping bag out to air and place all your bits on the ground sheet and pack up outside. If it is raining, then the whole procedure must be planned if the contents of your rucksack are going to stay dry.

The first thing to do is pack everything up into stuff sacks ready for rucksack entry. When everything is ready, try and pack your rucksack as best you can inside the tent. It can be done, but organisation is the key. Then get your boots and gaiters on and unhook the inner tent from the outer and pack that away. Up until this point, you will have been under cover and protected from the weather. All that is left to do is to take the fly down. Before you get outside, make sure your boots are adjusted and you have the right clothing under your waterproofs for walking in the rain; then do up your waterproofs, face the rain and finally pack your last piece of gear away, the tent flysheet.

That brings me back to the beginning of the chapter. Shoulder the pack up, get it comfortable for the day's travel and make sure the site is left in perfect condition. As you walk away from the pitch, you should be able to challenge anyone to try and prove that you have spent the night there — and win!

9
A Backpacking Adventure

This particular backpacking adventure was to take place soon after Christmas. For me, a five-day winter backpack with the likelihood of snow and ice. My friend was going to go up a few days earlier as he had the whole week free. We were going to meet at a particular camp site. The selected area was the Lake District.

We had planned this trip to a tee, with many evenings of route planning and getting equipment together, new and old, so as to cope with the conditions we were likely to come across. I was getting there by rail and bus; my friend was to motor up. Then we were going to travel home together in his car.

Having spent the last few hours of the night before getting my pack to a standard and lightness I had never thought possible for the expected conditions, I got up at four o'clock in the morning with as much enthusiasm as I could muster so early in the day. A hurried breakfast and I was soon on the train for Penrith.

I arrived at Penrith — the peaks were white! — and as I stepped out on to the platform I felt a barrier of cold air hit me like a snowball. The temperature difference compared with down south was considerable. I hurriedly walked to the bus station, only stopping for some chocolate bars as my connection was due to leave very soon. The bus driver-conductor commented that it was quite cool, not cold but cool. From the bus I had a superb view of the scenery, the Skiddaw range. Blencathra was draped in snow and it made me shiver just to look at it. On arrival in Keswick, a delightful lakeland town (with even a Chinese Takeaway I noticed) I changed bus for my destination, through the jaws of Borrowdale into Seathwaite. I arrived at the camp site where I was to meet up with my friend. He was erecting his tent as I stomped in.

After we had set up camp we cooked our evening meals. Mine was a new boil-in-the-bag curry and rice and my friend's an add-boiling-water-and-wait liver and onion mix. We drank our after-dinner brews as it got dark and then strolled up to the dale head before turning in for the night. It rained heavily during the night. I woke at first light to the sound of my friend's petrol stove roaring away and was immediately eager to know whether the snow had been melted by the heavy rainfall. I unzipped my fly sheet and looked outside, but the tops were covered in mist. I silently hoped that the snow still covered the hills. I ate breakfast and we were soon packed up, ready to go. We paid the site owner and started to walk. Our destination was either Sprinkling Tarn or Sty Head Tarn where we intended to pitch that night. Our plan was to do as many peaks as possible, so there was no sense in rushing the first day; besides we had had a late start and it starts getting dark before four o'clock up there.

When we reached Stockly Bridge we had a choice of the Styhead pass or the rather indirect Grains Gill route, which Wainwright said was more exciting. Wainwright's word was good enough for us, so it was Grains Gill. The long climb seemed to take far longer than it should have done. Mind you, we brewed and had a second breakfast which, of course, took time. We eventually got to the path junction after passing two ravines and crossing a stream. We were just below a mountain called Great End and at the top of the pass. One path led to a walled shelter and then on to Angle Tarn and the other down to

Sprinkling Tarn and then Styhead Tarn. We thought Sprinkling Tarn would make a good point for the overnight stop. By now, as we headed towards the Tarn we were walking on six inches of snow and ice and I began to thank God that the rain had not melted it; in fact the rain in the valley had probably turned to snow on the tops anyway. On arrival at Sprinkling Tarn the wind was gale force and, worse still, gusting. There was a Vango Force Ten tent pitched at the side of the tarn, with one side guy pulled out, but it was standing up to the wind quite happily even without a guy.

We searched every corner and every dip in and around the vicinity of the tarn for a sheltered pitch, but it was no use; the wind blew viciously at every point. My friend abandoned the search for a sheltered pitch and began to clear a flat piece of ground.

He had a proper mountain tent but I only had a semi-mountain tent, and was therefore very worried about pitching in such conditions. I wandered about for quite a while, looking and hoping, but nothing came up. As I walked back to my rucksack which was where my friend had started pitching his tent, I realised that I would have to pitch in this gale like it or not, and just hope for the best. As I undid the top of my rucksack to get my tent out, I looked up to where my friend was pitching his tent. Suddenly a terrific gust of wind got behind his flysheet, tore out the pegs and it started sailing like a kite towards a sheer edge close by. At first there seemed to be some hope of catching it, but directly after the first blow came a second gust which blew the fly right over the edge. We both rushed to the edge hoping it had caught on a rock, but there was no sign of it at all. My friend decided to go back down the path to see if he could get a glimpse of it and left his pack with me while he ran down with his ice-axe in his hand.

My mind began to play games with me; it was getting dark and we were miles away from the nearest cottage. I zipped up my jacket, put my balaclava on, huddled up to the packs and

shivered. It was nearly dark before my friend returned ex-
hausted. In between deep breaths he said that he hadn't found
it and he thought it would be best to take the Angle Tarn path
and then down Rosset Gill into Langdale where we might find
accommodation.

I agreed, feeling that we should get off the mountain before
complete darkness. It was pitch dark by the time we got to
Angle Tarn. We had never done this path before and looking at
Rosset Gill on the map, I thought then that somehow we would
not get down that night. Our night vision enabled us to make
the top of Rosset Gill, but as we descended this steep, rocky
and dangerous gully I smelt danger. Every other step we slipped and we could only progress very slowly. As we descended
further down we somehow lost the path and with every step the
situation got more nightmarish. After a climb up one side of the
gill in the hope of finding the path and a very dangerous des-
cent in which I nearly slipped over a very nasty edge, we both
decided to stay put and spend the night bivouacking.

We soon found some rocks which looked suitable for building our bivvy around and after about half an hour of building
side walls out of stones from up the gill our little home for the
night began to look good. Luckily we both had a spare blanket,
of the waterproof and heat reflecting type, and by lying one on
the floor and draping the other over the top of our bivvy we
managed to protect ourselves from the main elements. Before
we got in we put on every single piece of clothing we had so as
to keep as warm as possible through the long night ahead.

A full fourteen hours had to be spent out on a bleak mountain. I had my normal day clothing on plus two fibre-pile
jackets, a Gore-tex weatherproof suit, a pair of thick fibre-pile
mitts and a fully extended woollen balaclava, and I was still
cold as I tried to sleep. The wind blew relentlessly. If I asked
my friend the time once I must have asked him a dozen times.
There was no chance of getting to sleep and by midnight I was
so cold I began to worry. It began to snow heavily and I

decided to get out and move about and stay warm — Tony joined me. I worked a little bit on the bivvy and as we got back in again we decided that it might be dangerous to try to go to sleep, so we stayed awake chatting, shivering and rubbing ourselves and wiggling our toes to keep the circulation going. Tony suggested we light a candle. From then on the whole situation changed completely. As the little wax flame flickered we felt warm; we both stared into its depths as the hostile bivvy turned into a warm home just like magic. Until then I had not realised that such a simple object could give such a feeling of comfort. We gave up trying to sleep, in fact we no longer felt tired, even after the hard day's walking we had done. We chatted and laughed and felt great.

I got my meths stove, and thereafter time just flicked by with brew after brew and little treats like porridge, chocolate biscuits and oatmeal blocks. A further hitch did occur though; while it snowed hard a gust of wind blew the top space blanket completely off. I went outside to rebuild the top as Tony brewed yet again. When the bivvy was sound again and I prepared to get back in I noticed that every rock had something on it. One rock had our two mugs, the coffee bottle, a spoon and sweetener tablets on, another had all the snacks on, rationed out in rows. Tony was inside with the space blanket up around his legs looking with a half smile on his face, at the stove and the brew bubbling away. There were objects in every corner of our bivvy, making it look like Aladdin's cave.

At one point I had longed for dawn but as it slowly got lighter and lighter I didn't want to get out. Before we knew it our potentially dangerous situation was over and we were packed up and walking down to the Langdale valley.

I learnt a lot from this experience. We had made the best out of the situation and turned a pretty miserable outlook into something enjoyable that I certainly won't forget. But isn't that what backpacking is about?

Even experts make mistakes, although in my view there are

a

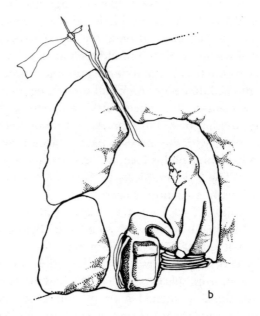

b

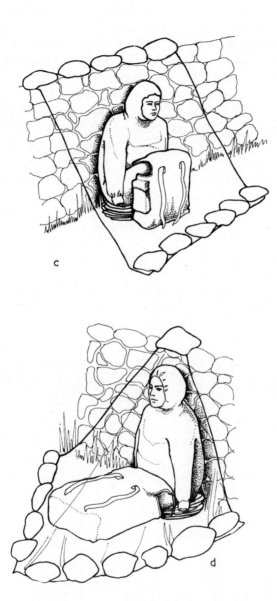

Bivouacking techniques: (a) inside a plastic bag with hole cut for face (b) snow hole with a signal projecting through the ventilation hole (c) lean-to method (d) wedge method

no such people as expert backpackers. Veteran backpackers still learn from trips: new ideas for comfort and cutting weight. And the quest for the perfect pack goes on.

I hope you have enjoyed this book and gathered something of the excitement that I feel for backpacking. But above all I hope that I have inspired you to get out in some corner of Britain and backpack yourself. Backpacking means so many different things to different people, but when the bug hits you will be able to say, 'Now I know what backpacking is all about'.

Appendix 1
Books and Magazines

INSTRUCTIONAL

Adshead, R. *Backpacking in Britain* (Oxford Ill. Press, 1974)
— — *The Spur Book of Backpacking* (Spurbooks, 1977)
Blackshaw, A. *Mountaineering* (Kaye & Ward, 1968)
Booth, D. *Backpacker's Handbook* (Hale, 1979)
Disley, J. *Tackle Climbing this Way* (S.Paul, 1977)
Greenbank, A. *Walking, Hiking and Backpacking* (Constable, 1977)
Jackson, J. *Safety on Mountains* (BMC, 1975)
Lumley, P. *The Spur Book Of Hill Trekking* (Spurbooks, 1976)
Venture Series (Spurbooks)
Winnett, T. *Backpacking for Fun* (Wilderness, 1972)

ADDITIONAL INTEREST

Langmuir, E. *Mountain Leadership* (Scottish Sports Council, 1969)
March, B. *Modern Snow and Ice Techniques* (Cicerone Press, 1973)
Milliner, C.D. *Mountain Photography* (Focal Press, 1977)
The Observer Book of Weather — Birds — Trees — Geology — Fungi
(Warne)
Unsworth, W. *Walking and Climbing* (Routledge, 1977)

GUIDES

Falconer, A. *The Cleveland Way* (HMSO, 1969)
Hillaby, J. *Journey Through Britain* (Constable, 1968; Paladin, 1970)
— — *Journey Through Europe* (Constable, 1972; Paladin, 1974)
HMSO National Park Booklets

B—H

Moir, D.G. *Scottish Hill Tracks — South* and *North* (Bartholemew, 1975)

Richards, M. *Cotswolds Way* (Thornhill P. 1979)

— — *North Cornwall* (Thornhill P. 1976)

Stephenson, T. *The Pennine Way* (HMSO, 1969)

Wainwright, A. *Coast to Coast Walk* (Westmorland Gazette, 1973)

— — *Pennine Way Companion* (Westmorland Gazette, 1968)

— — *Pictorial Guide to Lakeland Fells* (Westmorland Gazette, 1950, '60, '62, '64, '66)

Ward K. and Mason J. *Coastal Walks* (C. Letts, 1977)

Westacott, H.D. *Guide to Walking the Ridgeway* (Footpath Pbns, 1978)

Wright, C.J. *The Pennine Way* (Constable, 1975)

Wright, N. *English Mountain Summits* (Hale, 1974)

All of the above-mentioned books can be found in the book departments of good climbing shops and many can be found in your local library, which is a particularly economical way to read.

MAGAZINES

Adventure Sports
Camping Magazine
Camping World
Climber and Rambler
The Great Outdoors
Mountain World
Practical Camper

Appendix 2
Equipment

A list of equipment that has been personally tested by the author or by backpacking friends.

TENTS

Karrimor Marathon S Mk II and Mk III
Ultimate Equipment Solo, Packer, Tramp, Super Tramp and 'The Tent'
Phoenix Fortress

RUCKSACKS

Camp Trial Ponderosa and Astral Cruiser combination
Vango Super Ariel and Camp Trial Astral Cruiser combination
Berghaus Cyclops range of Anatomical Sacks
Karrimor Jaguar Mk II and Haston Alpinist
Lowe Alpine System range of sacks

SLEEPING BAGS

Mountain Equipment Snowline, Lightline and Laverado bags
Black Tromso and Norseland
Point Five Orion standard fibre-fill bag
Daimor Straithmor
The Vista range
The Ultimate range

COOKING EQUIPMENT

Trangia meths stove
Lyntham's Lightweight Titch gas stove
Vango Standard and Pre-heat gaz stoves
Camping gaz Bluet 2000 and Globe Trotter stove
Optimus SVEA petrol stove and 323 Petrol Stove

Trangia pots and pan
Lightline pot-pan set
Optimus lightweight billy set

BOOTS

Robert Lawrie range
Scarpa Monte Rosa and Bronzo models
Hawkins Helvellyn and Scafell models
Dolomite Vetta
James Boylan range
Nokia Bogtrotters

CLOTHING

Helly-Hansen Lifa underwear
Damart Thermo Polajamas
Helly-Hansen polar wear
Insulatawear body heaters
Javlin fibre-pile garments
Ultimate Equipment fibre-fill parka duvet
Henri Lloyd Glenco jacket and Orkney over-trousers
Berghaus Gore-tex weatherproofs
Hebden cord walking trousers
Belstaff Gore-tex clothing
Vista K2 fibre jacket
Rohan Halenca Super Striders and Super Solopettes
Shipmate fibre-pile wear
Tog 24 fibre-pile wear
Slater range of duvets
White Rock Fila range of mountain clothing
Peter Storm W1 proofed woollen sweater

ODDMENTS

Space blanket
Adsmat
French-made candle lantern
Meta brewing cup
Karrimat
Green-topped polybottle
Optimus fuel bottle
Chouinard frost ice-axe
Selewa instep crampons
Selewa adjustable crampons
Silva 15 TDCL compass
Standard climbing woollen balaclava
Insulatawear balaclava
Insulatawear mitts
Karrimor ski pouch

Appendix 3
Manufacturers

A.B. Optimus Ltd
(stoves)
Mill Road
Sharnbrook 1
Bedford

Belstaff Ltd
(outdoor clothing, Gore-tex)
Caroline Street
Longton
Stoke-on-Trent
Staffs

Berghaus
(clothing, rucksacks, boots)
34 Dean Street
Newcastle-upon-Tyne

Camp Trials
(rucksacks)
Waterford Industrial Estate
Ireland

Daimor
(sleeping bags)
75 Holland Street
Manchester

Fjällräven
Maclarens
Markington
Harrogate
Yorks

Helly-Hansen
(fibre-pile clothing, weather-proofs)
Ronald Close
Kempston,
Bedford.

Insulatawear Ltd
(fibre-pile clothing)
127 Old Street
Clevedon
Avon

Karrimor International Ltd
(tents, rucksacks, stoves)
19 Avenue Parade
Accrington
Lancs

Mountain Equipment
(sleeping bags, extreme-weather clothing)
George Street
Glossop, Derbys

Point Five
(sleeping bags, duvets)
Bantoms
Meadow Lane
Nottingham

Ranch House
(dried foods)
Greatham
Liss
Hants

Raven
(dried foods)
23 Oxenden Road
Arthingworth
Market Harborough
Leics

Rohan
(outdoor clothing)
3 Brook Street
Skipton
North Yorks

Springlow
(dried foods)
Marsland Mills
Green Street
Oldham
Lancs

Swelfoods
(dried foods)
Dawnedge
Aspley Guise
Milton Keynes

Ultimate Equipment Ltd
(tents, clothing, climbing gear)
Willowburn Trading Estate
The Butts
Warkworth
Morpeth
Northumbria

Vango
(tents, stoves, rucksacks, boots)
356 Armulree Street
Glasgow

Vista Ltd
(fibre-pile equipment)
106 Eldon Street
Haxby Road
York

Appendix 4
Useful Addresses

The Backpacker's Club
20 St Michaels Road
Tilehurst
Berks

BMC
Crawford House
Precinct Centre
Booth Street East
Manchester

Camping Club of Great Britain
(Lightweight or Mountaineering
Section)
11 Lower Grosvenor Place
London SW1

The Countryside Commission
Cambridge Gate
London NW1

Red Cross
14 Grosvenor Crescent
London SW1

Sports Council
70 Brompton Road
London SW3

Youth Hostels Association
Trevelyan House
8 St Stephen's Hill
St Albans
Hertfordshire

Appendix 5
Recommended Dried Food Packs

All Batchelor catering packs

Springlow Space Age:
  Beef mince with gravy
  Liver with onion gravy
  Chicken casserole
  One portion potato pack

Raven Peak Meals:
  Rice and curry
  Savory risotto
  Pasta and vegetable bolognaise
  Vegetable stew
  Custard and banana mix
  Strawberry and apple mix
  Rice pudding
  Savoury fry
  Scrambled egg

Raven Regal Meals:
  Shrimp curry with rice
  Chicken with rice
  Savoury beef with potato

Swel rapid apple mix

Index

123